NINJA CREAMi COOKBOOK WITH FULL COLOR PICTURES

2100 Mouthwatering Homemade Frozen Treats for Beginners and Advanced Users | Recipes for Irresistible Ice Cream, Sorbet, Gelato, Milkshakes, Smoothie Bowls, Mix-Ins, and More.

Cynthia Blanchette

Table of Contents

Introduction

The love affair between humans and frozen treats dates back thousands of years. The earliest records suggest that the Chinese were among the first to create a form of ice cream using a mixture of milk and rice packed in snow. The concept of frozen desserts traveled along the Silk Road. Eventually, it reached the Mediterranean, where the Greeks and Romans adopted the idea of using honey and fruit juices to flavor snow.

Fast forward to the Renaissance period, and we find that frozen desserts had become a luxury enjoyed by the elite in Italy and France. It wasn't until the 18th century that ice cream became more accessible to the general public, thanks to technological advancements in refrigeration. Today, ice cream and its many variations—gelato, sorbet, milkshakes, and more—are enjoyed by people of all ages, across cultures and continents.

In the modern era, the art of making ice cream has been revolutionized by innovative machines that bring the ice cream parlor into your kitchen. One such marvel is the Ninja NC301 CREAMi Ice Cream Maker. This compact yet powerful machine is designed to transform your frozen treat-making experience, offering a range of options from traditional ice creams to health-conscious alternatives.

The Ninja NC301 CREAMi comes packed with features that make it a standout choice for any frozen treat enthusiast. With an 800-watt motor and a voltage of 120 volts, this machine can turn almost anything into ice cream, sorbet, milkshakes, and more. The Ninja CREAMi gives you total control over your ingredients, allowing for a range of options from decadent gelato to low-sugar, keto, dairy-free, and vegan treats. Choose between Ice Cream, Sorbet, Gelato, Milkshake, Smoothie Bowl, Lite Ice Cream, and Mix-in settings for the perfect speed, pressure, and time combination. This unique feature enables the CREAMi to break down a uniform frozen block into an incredibly smooth, creamy texture. Creating a treat is as simple as prepping your base, freezing it overnight, and then processing it in the machine. All containers, lids, and paddles are top-rack dishwasher safe, making cleanup a breeze.

While many ice cream makers are on the market, the Ninja NC301 CREAMi sets itself apart in several key ways; Most ice cream makers specialize in one or two types of frozen treats. The Ninja CREAMi, however, offers seven different programs, making it one of the most versatile machines available. The ability to control every aspect of your frozen treat, from ingredients to texture, is something that few other machines offer. This patented technology is unique to Ninja and ensures that your ice creams and sorbets have a texture that rivals commercial brands. Despite its range of features, the Ninja CREAMi is compact enough to fit comfortably on your countertop, making it perfect for kitchens of all sizes.

In summary, the Ninja NC301 CREAMi Ice Cream Maker is not just another kitchen appliance; it's a gateway to a world of frozen delights limited only by your imagination. As you delve into the recipes in this book, you'll discover how to make the most of this incredible machine, creating frozen treats that are as unique as you are.

Getting Started with your CREAMi

Before you embark on your journey to create mouthwatering frozen treats with your Ninja NC301 CREAMi Ice Cream Maker, there are a few essentials you need to know. This section will guide you through the commonly used ingredients, the tools and equipment you'll need, and some safety tips to ensure your ice cream-making experience is both enjoyable and safe.

Ingredients Commonly Used

The beauty of making your own frozen treats is the freedom to choose high-quality, fresh ingredients. Here's a rundown of what you'll often use:

- **Dairy**: Whole milk, heavy cream, and condensed milk are the backbone of many ice cream recipes.

- **Sweeteners**: Popular choices include granulated sugar, honey, and maple syrup. For low-sugar options, consider stevia or monk fruit sweetener.

- **Flavorings**: Vanilla extract, cocoa powder, and fruit purees can add depth and complexity to your recipes.

- **Mix-ins**: Think chocolate chips, crushed cookies, fruit chunks, and even spices like cinnamon or nutmeg.

- **Specialty Ingredients**: For vegan or dairy-free options, you might use coconut milk, almond milk, or oat milk. Xanthan gum or guar gum can be used as stabilizers.

Tools and Equipment Needed

- **Ninja NC301 CREAMi Ice Cream Maker**: This is the star of the show. Make sure you've read the user manual and are familiar with all its functions.

- **Mixing Bowls**: For preparing your ice cream base and mix-ins.

- **Measuring Cups and Spoons**: Accurate measurements are crucial for the perfect consistency and flavor.

- **Spatula**: For mixing and transferring your ice cream base.

- **Ice Cream Scoop**: For serving your delicious creations.

- **Storage Containers**: Preferably with airtight lids to store any leftover ice cream.

Safety Tips

- **Read the Manual**: Always read the user manual for your Ninja NC301 CREAMi Ice Cream Maker to understand its operational guidelines and safety measures.

- **Electrical Safety**: Ensure the machine is placed on a stable surface away from water. Always unplug when not in use.

- **Hygiene**: Wash all tools and your hands thoroughly before starting. Make sure also to clean the ice cream maker parts that come in contact with food.

- **Temperature**: Always use cold ingredients. This improves the texture and minimizes the risk of bacterial growth.

- **Children**: If kids are involved, ensure they are supervised, especially when the machine is operating.

Basic Techniques
Preparing the Base

The foundation of any great frozen treat is a well-prepared base. Ice creams and gelatos usually involve a mixture of milk, cream, sugar, and flavorings. Sorbets, on the other hand, often require a simple syrup combined with fruit puree. Here are some key points to remember:

1. **Temperature**: Always start with cold ingredients. This helps in achieving a smoother texture.

2. **Mixing**: Use a whisk to mix the ingredients until the sugar is completely dissolved thoroughly.

3. **Straining**: For fruit-based recipes, strain the mixture to remove any seeds or pulp.

4. **Aging**: For a creamier texture, let the base sit in the refrigerator for at least 4 hours before processing.

Using the 7 One-Touch Programs

The Ninja NC301 CREAMi offers seven one-touch programs that make it incredibly easy to create a variety of frozen treats. Here's a quick guide:

1. **Ice Cream**: For traditional ice creams with a creamy, rich texture.

2. **Sorbet**: Ideal for fruit-based, dairy-free options.

3. **Gelato**: Produces a denser and more intensely flavored treat.

4. **Milkshake**: For thick, sippable treats.

5. **Smoothie Bowl**: Creates a thicker, spoonable smoothie.

6. **Lite Ice Cream**: For those watching their calories or sugar intake.

7. **Mix-in**: Use this setting to blend in your favorite toppings like chocolate chips or fruit pieces.

Customizing with Mix-ins

One of the joys of using the Ninja NC301 CREAMi is the ability to customize your frozen treats with mix-ins. Here are some tips:

1. **Timing**: Add mix-ins during the last few minutes of churning to ensure even distribution.

2. **Size**: Chop your mix-ins into small, bite-sized pieces for a better texture.

3. **Variety**: Don't limit yourself to just one; try combining multiple mix-ins like chocolate and nuts.

4. **Experiment**: From fresh fruits to cookie crumbs, the possibilities are endless.

Re-spin Function

The Re-spin function on the Ninja NC301 CREAMi is a game-changer. If you find that your frozen treat isn't as soft or creamy as you'd like, simply select the Re-spin function. This will reprocess the mixture, breaking down ice crystals and resulting in a smoother, creamier texture. Here's how to use it:

1. **Check Consistency**: After the initial spin, check the texture of your treat.

2. **Select Re-spin**: If it's not to your liking, select the Re-spin function.

3. **Process**: The machine will re-churn the mixture.

4. **Enjoy**: Your frozen treat should now have the perfect texture.

Tips and Tricks
How to Use Creamify Technology for Best Results

The Ninja CREAMi Ice Cream Maker is equipped with Creamify Technology, which ensures your frozen treats turn out incredibly smooth and creamy. Here's how to make the most of it:

1. **Pre-Chill Ingredients**: Before you start, make sure your base ingredients (cream, milk, sugar, etc.) are properly chilled. This helps Creamify Technology work more effectively and results in a smoother texture.

2. **Uniform Mixing**: Ensure that you mix your ingredients thoroughly before pouring them into the CREAMi Pint. Even distribution of ingredients contributes to a consistent and creamy texture.

3. **Freeze Overnight**: After preparing your ice cream base, freeze it in the CREAMi Pint for a minimum of 4 hours, or ideally, overnight. This extended freezing time allows Creamify Technology to work its magic and transform your mixture into a velvety delight.

4. **Correct Paddle Placement**: When using the Ninja CREAMi, ensure that the Creamerizer Paddle is securely installed. Proper paddle placement is crucial for achieving the desired texture.

5. **Follow One-Touch Programs**: Utilize the convenience of the one-touch programs available on the Ninja CREAMi. These programs are designed to optimize the combination of speed, pressure, and time for each specific frozen treat category, ensuring consistently delicious results.

Ideas for Mix-Ins

Customizing your ice cream with mix-ins adds a fun and personalized touch to your frozen creations. Here are some ideas to get your creative juices flowing:

1. **Chocolate Lovers' Dream**: Add chunks of your favorite chocolate bars, brownie pieces, or chocolate chips for a rich and indulgent chocolate experience.

2. **Fruity Delights**: Incorporate fresh fruit pieces like berries, mango, or banana slices for a burst of natural sweetness and refreshing flavor.

3. **Nutty Crunch**: Crushed nuts such as almonds, pecans, or walnuts provide a satisfying crunch and a delightful contrast to creamy ice cream.

4. **Cookie Extravaganza**: Crushed cookies, from classic chocolate chip to sandwich cookies like Oreo, make for an irresistible ice cream mix-in.

5. **Candy Galore**: Go wild with candy additions like gummy bears, M&M's, or caramel swirls for a playful and colorful twist.

6. **Spices and Flavors**: Experiment with spices like cinnamon or nutmeg, or explore unique flavorings like lavender or cardamom for a sophisticated taste.

Troubleshooting Common Issues

Encountering issues while making ice cream is common, but here are some troubleshooting tips to help you out:

1. **Ice Crystals**: If your ice cream turns icy, ensure that your ice cream base was properly mixed and chilled before processing. Over-churning can also lead to ice crystals, so monitor the processing time.

2. **Too Soft**: If your ice cream is too soft, try freezing it for a bit longer in the CREAMi Pint before serving. Also, double-check that the Creamerizer Paddle is properly attached.

3. **Not Creamy Enough**: To achieve a creamier texture, use the Re-spin function on the Ninja CREAMi if your ice cream isn't as smooth as you'd like after the initial processing.

4. **Flavor Balance**: Adjust the amount of mix-ins or flavorings to achieve your desired taste. Sometimes, less is more when it comes to creating a balanced flavor profile.

5. **Uneven Mix-Ins**: Ensure that you evenly distribute your mix-ins throughout the ice cream base to avoid clumping in certain areas.

With these tips and tricks, you'll be able to create a wide variety of delectable frozen treats using your Ninja CREAMi Ice Cream Maker. Happy ice cream making!

Ice Creams

Classic Vanilla Ice Cream

SERVES 4

There's nothing quite like the timeless allure of Classic Vanilla Ice Cream. Remarkably, this recipe achieves a level of creaminess and richness without any egg yolks. Classic Vanilla is a versatile favorite that never goes out of style.

PREP TIME: 10 minutes / Freeze time: 4 hours

FUNCTION: Ice Cream

TOOLS NEEDED: Mixing bowl, whisk or rubber spatula

Ingredients

- 2 cups of heavy cream
- 1 cup of whole milk
- 3/4 cup of granulated sugar
- 1 vanilla bean, split and seeds scraped
- 1 teaspoon pure vanilla extract

Instructions

1. In a bowl, mix the heavy cream, whole milk, and granulated sugar. Whip the sugar until completely dissolved.

2. Add the scraped seeds from the vanilla bean and the pure vanilla extract to the mixture. Stir until well combined.

3. Transfer the mixture to a CREAMi Pint, seal it with the storage lid, and place it in the freezer for a minimum of 4 hours. This chilling period is essential for achieving the desired creamy texture.

4. After the freezing time, take the CREAMi Pint out and remove the lid. Put the CREAMi pint in the outer bowl, ensuring the Creamerizer Paddle is attached onto the lid of the outer bowl, and lock.

5. Position the bowl onto the base and turn the handle towards the right in order to secure it. Select the Ice Cream function to begin churning.

6. As soon as the churning process is completed, your Classic Vanilla Ice Cream is ready to be enjoyed. Serve it immediately with your favorite toppings, or let its pure, unadulterated flavor shine on its own.

PREP TIP:

For an even richer vanilla flavor, consider using two vanilla beans.

Chocolate Fudge Ice Cream

SERVES 4

Indulge in the velvety richness of Chocolate Fudge Ice Cream. This irresistible treat combines chocolate's deep, luscious flavor with a fudgy texture that's a delight to the senses.

PREP TIME: 15 minutes / Freeze time: 4 hours

FUNCTION: Ice Cream

TOOLS NEEDED: Mixing bowl, whisk or rubber spatula

Ingredients

- 2 cups of heavy cream

- 1 cup of whole milk

- 1 cup granulated sugar

- 1/2 cup unsweetened cocoa powder

- 1/4 cup chocolate fudge sauce

Instructions

1. In a mixing bowl, blend together the heavy cream, whole milk, granulated sugar, and unsweetened cocoa powder until the sugar is fully dissolved.

2. Stir in the chocolate fudge sauce until the mixture is uniform and has a rich chocolatey hue.

3. Transfer the mixture to a CREAMi Pint and secure the lid. Freeze for at least 4 hours.

4. After freezing, insert the pint into your Ninja CREAMi machine. Attach the Creamerizer Paddle and select the Ice Cream function.

5. Once the cycle is complete, serve your Chocolate Fudge Ice Cream immediately for a truly indulgent dessert.

PREP TIP:

For a more intense chocolate flavor, consider using high-quality cocoa powder.

Strawberry Swirl Ice Cream

SERVES 4

Embrace the essence of summer with this luscious Strawberry Swirl Ice Cream. The sweet and tangy strawberry swirl complements the creamy base, making each bite a delightful experience.

PREP TIME: 20 minutes / Freeze time: 4 hours

FUNCTION: Ice Cream

TOOLS NEEDED: Mixing bowl, whisk or rubber spatula

Ingredients

- 2 cups of heavy cream
- 1 cup of whole milk
- 3/4 cup of granulated sugar
- 1 cup strawberry puree
- 1 teaspoon lemon juice

Instructions

1. In a bowl, mix the heavy cream, whole milk, and granulated sugar. Stir until the sugar is dissolved.

2. In a separate bowl, mix the strawberry puree and lemon juice.

3. Gently fold the strawberry mixture into the cream mixture to create a swirl effect.

4. Transfer the swirled mixture to a CREAMi Pint and secure the lid. Freeze for at least 4 hours.

5. After freezing, place the pint into your Ninja CREAMi machine. Attach the Creamerizer Paddle and select the Ice Cream function.

6. Once the cycle is complete, serve your Strawberry Swirl Ice Cream as is or garnish with fresh strawberries if desired.

PREP TIP:

For an even more vibrant flavor, use ripe, in-season strawberries for the puree.

Mint Chocolate Chip Ice Cream

SERVES 4

This Mint Chocolate Chip Ice Cream offers a refreshing and delightful combination of cool mint and rich chocolate chips. It's the perfect treat for a hot summer day or any time you crave a classic flavor pairing.

PREP TIME: 10 minutes / Freeze time: 4 hours

FUNCTION: Ice Cream

TOOLS NEEDED: Mixing bowl, whisk or rubber spatula

Ingredients

- 2 cups of heavy cream
- 1 cup of whole milk
- 3/4 cup of granulated sugar
- 1 teaspoon peppermint extract
- 1/2 cup mini chocolate chips

Instructions

1. In a bowl, mix the heavy cream, whole milk, and granulated sugar. Stir until the sugar is dissolved.

2. Add the peppermint extract to the mixture and stir until well combined.

3. Transfer the mixture to a CREAMi Pint and add the mini chocolate chips. Secure the lid and freeze for at least 4 hours.

4. After freezing, place the pint into your Ninja CREAMi machine. Attach the Creamerizer Paddle and select the Ice Cream function.

5. Once the cycle is complete, serve your Mint Chocolate Chip Ice Cream immediately, garnished with fresh mint leaves if desired.

PREP TIP:

For a more intense mint flavor, you can add a few drops of green food coloring or use fresh mint leaves for garnish.

Cookies and Cream Ice Cream

SERVES 4

Cookies and Cream Ice Cream is a beloved favorite that marries the satisfying crunch of chocolate sandwich cookies with velvety ice cream. This classic flavor is sure to please the whole family.

PREP TIME: 10 minutes / Freeze time: 4 hours

FUNCTION: Ice Cream

TOOLS NEEDED: Mixing bowl, whisk or rubber spatula

Ingredients

- 2 cups of heavy cream
- 1 cup of whole milk
- 3/4 cup of granulated sugar
- 10 chocolate sandwich cookies, crushed

Instructions

1. In a bowl, mix the heavy cream, whole milk, and granulated sugar. Stir until the sugar is dissolved.

2. Add the crushed chocolate sandwich cookies to the mixture and stir until they are evenly distributed.

3. Transfer the mixture to a CREAMi Pint and secure the lid. Freeze for at least 4 hours.

4. After freezing, place the pint into your Ninja CREAMi machine. Attach the Creamerizer Paddle and select the Ice Cream function.

5. Once the cycle is complete, serve your Cookies and Cream Ice Cream, allowing the delightful cookie bits to provide a delightful crunch in each bite.

PREP TIP:

Feel free to customize the level of cookie crunchiness by adjusting the cookie pieces to your preference.

Salted Caramel Ice Cream

SERVES 4

Salted Caramel Ice Cream offers a harmonious blend of sweet and salty flavors, creating a dessert experience that's both rich and intriguing. The contrast between the buttery caramel and a touch of sea salt makes every spoonful a delight.

PREP TIME: 15 minutes / Freeze time: 4 hours

FUNCTION: Ice Cream

TOOLS NEEDED: Mixing bowl, whisk or rubber spatula

Ingredients

- 2 cups of heavy cream

- 1 cup of whole milk

- 3/4 cup of granulated sugar

- 1/2 cup caramel sauce (homemade or store-bought)

- 1/2 teaspoon sea salt (adjust to taste)

Instructions

1. In a bowl, mix the heavy cream, whole milk, and granulated sugar. Stir until the sugar is dissolved.

2. Add the caramel sauce and sea salt to the mixture. Adjust the amount of sea salt to your taste preference, keeping in mind that it should provide a subtle contrast to the sweetness of the caramel.

3. Mix the ingredients until the caramel and sea salt are fully incorporated.

4. Transfer the mixture to a CREAMi Pint and secure the lid. Freeze for at least 4 hours, allowing the flavors to meld.

5. After freezing, place the pint into your Ninja CREAMi machine. Attach the Creamerizer Paddle and select the Ice Cream function.

6. Once the cycle is complete, serve your Salted Caramel Ice Cream. The combination of creamy caramel and a hint of salt will leave your taste buds dancing.

PREP TIP:

For added texture, you can drizzle extra caramel sauce on top before serving.

Butter Pecan Ice Cream

SERVES 4

Butter Pecan Ice Cream is a classic favorite known for its rich, buttery flavor and the delightful crunch of toasted pecans. This recipe captures the essence of this beloved dessert, ensuring that every spoonful is a delectable experience.

PREP TIME: 15 minutes / Freeze time: 4 hours

FUNCTION: Ice Cream

TOOLS NEEDED: Mixing bowl, whisk or rubber spatula, baking sheet

Ingredients

- 2 cups of heavy cream
- 1 cup of whole milk
- 3/4 cup of granulated sugar
- 1/2 cup unsalted butter
- 1 cup pecan halves
- 1 teaspoon pure vanilla extract

Instructions

1. Begin by toasting the pecans for that wonderful crunch. Preheat your oven to 350°F (175°C). Place the pecan halves on a baking sheet and toast them in the oven for about 7-10 minutes or until they turn golden and fragrant. Be sure to keep an eye on them to prevent over-browning. Once toasted, remove them from the oven and let them cool. Then roughly chop them into smaller pieces.

2. In a bowl, mix the heavy cream, whole milk, and granulated sugar. Whip the sugar until completely dissolved.

3. In a separate microwave-safe bowl, melt the unsalted butter. Allow it to cool slightly before adding it to the cream mixture. Stir well to incorporate the butter.

4. Add the toasted and chopped pecans to the mixture, reserving a handful for garnish if desired. Stir them in, ensuring they are evenly distributed.

5. Finally, add the pure vanilla extract and stir until everything is well combined.

6. Transfer the mixture to a CREAMi Pint, seal it with the storage lid, and place it in the freezer for at least 4 hours. This step is crucial for achieving the ideal texture and flavor.

7. After the freezing time, remove the CREAMi Pint out of the freezer, then take off the lid. Put the CREAMi pint in the outer bowl, ensuring the Creamerizer Paddle is attached onto the lid of the outer bowl, and lock.

8. Position the bowl onto the base and turn the handle towards the right in order to secure it. Select the Ice Cream function to begin churning.

9. Once the machine completes the churning process, your Butter Pecan Ice Cream is ready to be enjoyed. Serve it immediately, garnished with reserved pecans if desired.

PREP TIP:

Toasting the pecans enhances their flavor and adds a delightful crunch to the ice cream. Be careful not to over-toast them.

Coconut Cream Ice Cream

SERVES 4

Coconut Cream Ice Cream offers a delightful tropical escape in every spoonful. The creamy coconut flavor and velvety texture make this dessert a true indulgence.

PREP TIME: 10 minutes / Freeze time: 4 hours

FUNCTION: Ice Cream

TOOLS NEEDED: Mixing bowl, whisk or rubber spatula

Ingredients

- 2 cups coconut cream
- 1 cup coconut milk
- 3/4 cup of granulated sugar

- 1/2 cup shredded coconut

- 1 teaspoon pure coconut extract

Instructions

1. In a mixing bowl, combine the coconut cream, coconut milk, and granulated sugar. Whip the sugar until completely dissolved.

2. Add the shredded coconut and pure coconut extract to the mixture. Stir until well combined.

3. Transfer the mixture to a CREAMi Pint, seal it with the storage lid, and place it in the freezer for a minimum of 4 hours. This chilling period is crucial for achieving the desired creamy texture.

4. After the freezing time, take the CREAMi Pint out and remove the lid. Put the CREAMi pint in the outer bowl, ensuring the Creamerizer Paddle is attached onto the lid of the outer bowl, and lock.

5. Position the bowl onto the base and turn the handle towards the right in order to secure it. Select the Ice Cream function to begin churning.

6. As soon as the churning process is completed, your Coconut Cream Ice Cream is ready to be enjoyed. Serve it immediately, garnished with extra shredded coconut if desired, for an extra tropical touch.

PREP TIP:

For a more intense coconut flavor, consider adding a touch more pure coconut extract to suit your taste.

Matcha Green Tea Ice Cream

SERVES 4

Matcha Green Tea Ice Cream offers a unique and refreshing twist to the world of frozen desserts. With its vibrant green color and earthy, slightly bitter flavor, it's a delightful treat for those who appreciate the taste of matcha.

PREP TIME: 15 minutes / Freeze time: 4 hours

FUNCTION: Ice Cream

TOOLS NEEDED: Mixing bowl, whisk or rubber spatula

Ingredients

- 2 cups of heavy cream
- 1 cup of whole milk
- 3/4 cup of granulated sugar
- 2 tablespoons high-quality matcha green tea powder
- 1 teaspoon pure vanilla extract

Instructions

1. In a bowl, mix the heavy cream, whole milk, and granulated sugar. Stir until the sugar is completely dissolved.

2. Gradually add the matcha green tea powder to the mixture. Use a whisk or rubber spatula to thoroughly incorporate it. This step ensures the vibrant green color and distinct matcha flavor.

3. Stir in the pure vanilla extract until the mixture is well blended.

4. Transfer the matcha-infused mixture to a CREAMi Pint and seal it with the storage lid. Place the pint in the freezer for a minimum of 4 hours. This freezing time allows the ice cream to set and intensifies the matcha flavor.

5. After the freezing period, remove the CREAMi Pint out of the freezer, then take off the lid. Put the CREAMi pint in the outer bowl. Ensure that the Creamerizer Paddle is attached to the lid of the outer bowl and lock the assembly into place.

6. Position the bowl onto the base and turn the handle towards the right in order to secure it. Select the Ice Cream function to initiate the churning process.

7. Once the machine has finished churning, your Matcha Green Tea Ice Cream is ready to be enjoyed. Serve it immediately as a delightful dessert or enjoy it on its own to savor the unique matcha experience.

PREP TIP:

For an even more vibrant green color, consider using ceremonial-grade matcha powder.

Black Raspberry Ice Cream

SERVES 4

Black Raspberry Ice Cream is a delightful fusion of vibrant fruitiness and creamy indulgence. This recipe captures the essence of ripe black raspberries, resulting in a lusciously purple-hued dessert that's both refreshing and satisfying.

PREP TIME: 15 minutes / Freeze time: 4 hours

FUNCTION: Ice Cream

TOOLS NEEDED: Mixing bowl, whisk or rubber spatula

Ingredients

- 2 cups fresh or frozen black raspberries
- 1 cup granulated sugar
- 2 cups of heavy cream
- 1 cup of whole milk
- 1 teaspoon pure vanilla extract
- 1 tablespoon lemon juice

Instructions

1. Begin by preparing the black raspberry puree. If using fresh raspberries, rinse them thoroughly. If using frozen raspberries, allow them to thaw.

2. In a mixing bowl, combine the black raspberries and granulated sugar. Mash and stir the berries until they break down and release their juices. This will create a vibrant raspberry puree.

3. In a separate mixing bowl, whisk together the heavy cream, whole milk, pure vanilla extract, and lemon juice.

4. Combine the raspberry puree with the creamy mixture. Stir until everything is thoroughly incorporated, creating a beautiful purple-hued base.

5. Transfer the raspberry-infused ice cream base to a CREAMi Pint, seal it with the storage lid, and place it in the freezer for at least 4 hours. This resting period allows the flavors to meld and the texture to become wonderfully creamy.

6. After the freezing time, take the CREAMi Pint out and remove the lid. Put the CREAMi pint in the outer bowl, ensuring the Creamerizer Paddle is attached onto the lid of the outer bowl, and lock.

7. Position the bowl onto the base and turn the handle towards the right in order to secure it. Select the Ice Cream function to commence churning.

8. As soon as the churning process is completed, your Black Raspberry Ice Cream is ready to be enjoyed. Serve it immediately, savoring the vibrant fruitiness and creamy richness.

PREP TIP:

For an added burst of raspberry flavor, consider adding a handful of fresh black raspberries as a topping when serving.

Rum Raisin Ice Cream

SERVES 4

Indulge in the sophisticated and delightful flavors of Rum Raisin Ice Cream. This classic dessert combines the warmth of rum-soaked raisins with the creamy sweetness of ice cream. It's a truly special treat.

PREP TIME: 15 minutes / Freeze time: 4 hours

FUNCTION: Ice Cream

TOOLS NEEDED: Mixing bowl, whisk or rubber spatula, small saucepan

Ingredients

- 1/2 cup raisins
- 1/4 cup dark rum
- 2 cups of heavy cream
- 1 cup of whole milk
- 3/4 cup of granulated sugar
- 1 teaspoon pure vanilla extract

Instructions

1. Start by preparing the rum-soaked raisins. In a small saucepan, heat the dark rum over low heat until it's warm but not boiling. Remove it from the heat and add the raisins. Allow them to soak in the rum for at least 30 minutes. This step infuses the raisins with the rich, aromatic flavor of rum.

2. In a bowl, mix the heavy cream, whole milk, and granulated sugar. Whip the sugar until completely dissolved.

3. Add the pure vanilla extract to the mixture and stir until well combined.

4. After the raisins have soaked in the rum, drain them and gently pat them dry with a paper towel.

5. Chop the soaked raisins into smaller pieces to ensure an even distribution throughout the ice cream.

6. Add the chopped rum-soaked raisins to the cream mixture and stir to distribute them evenly.

7. Transfer the ice cream base to a CREAMi Pint, seal it with the storage lid, and place it in the freezer. Allow it to freeze for a minimum of 4 hours to achieve a delightful texture.

8. Once the freezing time is complete, take the CREAMi Pint out and remove the lid. Put the CREAMi pint in the outer bowl, ensuring the Creamerizer Paddle is attached onto the lid of the outer bowl, and lock.

9. Position the bowl onto the base and turn the handle towards the right in order to secure it. Select the Ice Cream function to start churning.

10. When the churning process is finished, your Rum Raisin Ice Cream is ready to be savored. Serve it as a delightful dessert, savoring each spoonful of creamy sweetness and the subtle warmth of rum-soaked raisins.

PREP TIP:

For an adult twist, you can increase the amount of dark rum for a more pronounced flavor.

Cherry Garcia Ice Cream

SERVES 4

Cherry Garcia Ice Cream is a beloved classic, known for its sweet cherries, rich chocolate chunks, and creamy base. This homemade version captures all the flavors you adore in this iconic ice cream.

PREP TIME: 15 minutes / Freeze time: 4 hours

FUNCTION: Ice Cream

TOOLS NEEDED: Mixing bowl, whisk or rubber spatula

Ingredients

- 2 cups of heavy cream

- 1 cup of whole milk
- 3/4 cup of granulated sugar
- 1 cup fresh or frozen cherries, pitted and halved
- 1/2 cup dark chocolate chunks or chips

Instructions

1. In a bowl, mix the heavy cream, whole milk, and granulated sugar. Whip the sugar until completely dissolved.

2. Gently fold in the pitted and halved cherries. Ensure they are evenly distributed throughout the mixture.

3. Add the dark chocolate chunks or chips, mixing until they are well incorporated into the base.

4. Transfer the ice cream mixture to a CREAMi Pint, seal it with the storage lid, and place it in the freezer for a minimum of 4 hours. This time is essential for the ice cream to freeze and the flavors to meld.

5. Once the freezing period is complete, retrieve the CREAMi Pint out of the freezer, then take off the lid. Put the CREAMi pint in the outer bowl, making sure the Creamerizer Paddle is attached onto the lid of the outer bowl, and lock.

6. Position the bowl components on the motor-base and secure by turning the handle to the right. Select the Ice Cream function to begin churning.

7. After the machine has finished churning, your homemade Cherry Garcia Ice Cream is ready to be savored. Serve it immediately, and enjoy the delightful combination of sweet cherries and decadent chocolate chunks.

PREP TIP:

For an even more intense chocolate experience, consider using dark chocolate chunks with a high cocoa content.

Tiramisu Ice Cream

SERVES 4

Indulge in the classic Italian dessert in frozen form with this delightful Tiramisu Ice Cream. It captures the essence of tiramisu with the rich flavors of coffee, cocoa, and mascarpone, all in a creamy ice cream.

PREP TIME: 15 minutes / Freeze time: 4 hours

FUNCTION: Ice Cream

TOOLS NEEDED: Mixing bowl, whisk or rubber spatula

Ingredients

- 2 cups of heavy cream
- 1 cup of whole milk
- 3/4 cup of granulated sugar
- 2 tablespoons instant coffee granules
- 2 tablespoons coffee liqueur (e.g., Kahlúa)
- 1/2 cup mascarpone cheese
- 1/4 cup unsweetened cocoa powder
- 1 teaspoon pure vanilla extract

Instructions

1. In a bowl, mix the heavy cream, whole milk, and granulated sugar. Whip the sugar until completely dissolved.

2. Add the instant coffee granules and coffee liqueur to the mixture. Stir until the coffee is well incorporated.

3. Gently fold in the mascarpone cheese until the mixture is smooth and creamy.

4. Add the unsweetened cocoa powder and pure vanilla extract. Mix until the cocoa is fully blended, creating a luscious mocha flavor.

5. Transfer the tiramisu ice cream base to a CREAMi Pint, seal it with the storage lid, and place it in the freezer for a minimum of 4 hours. This ensures a creamy and well-set ice cream.

6. After the freezing time, take the CREAMi Pint out and remove the lid. Put the CREAMi pint in the outer bowl. Ensure that the Creamerizer Paddle is attached to the outer bowl lid, and lock the lid assembly onto the outer bowl.

7. Position the bowl onto the base and turn the handle towards the right in order to secure it. Select the Ice Cream function to begin churning.

8. As soon as the churning process is completed, your Tiramisu Ice Cream is ready to enjoy. Serve it with a dusting of cocoa powder or a drizzle of coffee liqueur for that authentic tiramisu touch.

PREP TIP:

For an extra boost of coffee flavor, dissolve the instant coffee granules in a small amount of hot water before adding them to the mixture.

Cinnamon Roll Ice Cream

SERVES 4

Indulge in the sweet, spiced nostalgia of Cinnamon Roll Ice Cream. This delightful creation combines all the flavors of a classic cinnamon roll in a creamy, frozen treat.

PREP TIME: 15 minutes / Freeze time: 4 hours

FUNCTION: Ice Cream

TOOLS NEEDED: Mixing bowl, whisk or rubber spatula

Ingredients

- 2 cups of heavy cream
- 1 cup of whole milk
- 3/4 cup of granulated sugar
- 1 teaspoon ground cinnamon
- 1/4 cup chopped pecans (optional)
- 1/2 cup crushed cinnamon roll pieces (store-bought or homemade)
- 1 teaspoon pure vanilla extract
- 1/4 cup cream cheese frosting (store-bought or homemade)

Instructions

1. Combine in a mixing bowl the heavy cream, granulated sugar, whole milk , and ground cinnamon. Stir until the sugar is completely dissolved.

2. If you prefer a nutty crunch, add the chopped pecans to the mixture and stir until evenly distributed.

3. Gently fold in the crushed cinnamon roll pieces. These will infuse your ice cream with that signature cinnamon roll flavor.

4. Finally, incorporate the pure vanilla extract for an extra layer of aroma and taste.

5. Transfer the mixture to a CREAMi Pint, seal it with the storage lid, and place it in the freezer for at least 4 hours. This resting period ensures your ice cream has the perfect consistency.

6. Once the freezing time is up, take the CREAMi Pint out and remove the lid. Put the CREAMi pint in the outer bowl. Ensure the Creamerizer Paddle is attached to the lid of the outer bowl and lock the assembly into place.

7. Position the bowl assembly on the motor base and twist the handle to the right to raise the platform and lock it in place. Select the Ice Cream function to commence the churning process.

8. After the machine completes the churning, your Cinnamon Roll Ice Cream is ready to be savored.

9. As a finishing touch, drizzle your ice cream with cream cheese frosting for an authentic cinnamon roll experience.

10.   Serve immediately, and enjoy the delightful blend of cinnamon, cream, and sweetness in each scoop.

PREP TIP:

For homemade crushed cinnamon roll pieces, bake a cinnamon roll and let it cool completely before breaking it into small chunks.

Lavender Honey Ice Cream

SERVES 4

Lavender Honey Ice Cream is a delightful and fragrant treat that combines the soothing essence of lavender with the natural sweetness of honey. It's a unique and elegant flavor that's perfect for those seeking a refreshing twist on traditional ice cream.

PREP TIME: 15 minutes / Freeze time: 4 hours

FUNCTION: Ice Cream

TOOLS NEEDED: Mixing bowl, whisk or rubber spatula

Ingredients

- 2 cups of heavy cream

- 1 cup of whole milk

- 1/2 cup granulated sugar

- 2 tablespoons dried culinary lavender buds

- 1/3 cup honey (preferably floral honey)

- 1 teaspoon pure vanilla extract

Instructions

1. Begin by combining the heavy cream, whole milk, and granulated sugar in a mixing bowl. Whip the sugar until completely dissolved.

2. Add the dried culinary lavender buds to the mixture. Gently crush the buds between your fingers as you stir to release their aromatic flavor. Allow the mixture to infuse for about 10 minutes, ensuring that the lavender essence blends in.

3. After the infusion, strain the mixture through a fine-mesh sieve or cheesecloth to remove the lavender buds. Return the lavender-infused mixture to the mixing bowl.

4. Stir in the honey and pure vanilla extract until well combined. The honey will add a beautiful sweetness and a subtle floral note to the ice cream.

5. Transfer the lavender-honey mixture to a CREAMi Pint and seal it with the storage lid. Freeze for a minimum of 4 hours to achieve the desired creamy texture and allow the flavors to meld.

6. Once the freezing time is complete, take the CREAMi Pint out and remove the lid. Put the CREAMi pint in the outer bowl, ensuring that the Creamerizer Paddle is attached onto the lid of the outer bowl, and lock.

7. Position the bowl components on the motor-base and secure by turning the handle to the right. Select the Ice Cream function to begin churning.

8. After the churning process is complete, your Lavender Honey Ice Cream is ready to delight your taste buds. Serve it immediately, garnished with a fresh sprig of lavender for an extra touch of elegance.

PREP TIP:

Ensure you use culinary lavender, specifically intended for cooking, to maintain the best flavor and quality.

Peach Cobbler Ice Cream

SERVES 4

Indulge in the comforting flavors of a classic dessert with a twist - Peach Cobbler Ice Cream. This frozen delight combines the sweetness of ripe peaches with the warmth of cinnamon and a buttery streusel topping, all in a creamy ice cream base. It's like enjoying peach cobbler in frozen form!

PREP TIME: 15 minutes / Freeze time: 4 hours

FUNCTION: Ice Cream

TOOLS NEEDED: Mixing bowl, whisk or rubber spatula

Ingredients

- 2 cups of heavy cream
- 1 cup of whole milk
- 3/4 cup of granulated sugar
- 2 ripe peaches, peeled, pitted, and diced
- 1 teaspoon ground cinnamon
- 1 teaspoon pure vanilla extract

For the Streusel Topping:

- 1/2 cup all-purpose flour
- 1/4 cup brown sugar
- 1/4 cup unsalted butter, cold and cubed
- 1/2 teaspoon ground cinnamon

- Pinch of salt

Instructions

1. Begin by preparing the streusel topping. In a small bowl, combine the all-purpose flour, brown sugar, cold cubed butter, ground cinnamon, and a pinch of salt. Use a pastry cutter or your fingers to blend the ingredients until the mixture resembles coarse crumbs. Set this streusel aside.

2. In a bowl, mix the heavy cream, whole milk, and granulated sugar. Whip the sugar until completely dissolved.

3. Add the diced ripe peaches, ground cinnamon, and pure vanilla extract to the cream mixture. Stir until everything is well combined.

4. Transfer the mixture to a CREAMi Pint and seal it with the storage lid. Place it in the freezer for a minimum of 4 hours to allow the flavors to meld.

5. After the freezing time, take the CREAMi Pint out and remove the lid. Put the CREAMi pint in the outer bowl, ensuring the Creamerizer Paddle is attached onto the lid of the outer bowl, and lock.

6. Position the bowl components on the motor-base and secure by turning the handle to the right. Select the Ice Cream function to begin churning.

7. As the ice cream begins to form, sprinkle the streusel topping into the churned mixture in the final few minutes to incorporate the cobbler-like crunch.

8. Once the machine completes the churning process, your Peach Cobbler Ice Cream is ready to be savored. Serve it in bowls or cones, and enjoy the delightful combination of peaches, cinnamon, and streusel in every scoop.

PREP TIP:

For a more intense peach flavor, consider using slightly more ripe peaches.

Lemon Curd Ice Cream

SERVES 4

Lemon Curd Ice Cream is a citrusy delight that strikes the perfect balance between zesty and sweet. The bright and tangy flavors of lemon are beautifully complemented by the creaminess of this ice cream, making it a refreshing treat.

PREP TIME: 15 minutes / Freeze time: 4 hours

FUNCTION: Ice Cream

TOOLS NEEDED: Mixing bowl, whisk or rubber spatula

Ingredients

- 2 cups of heavy cream
- 1 cup of whole milk
- 3/4 cup of granulated sugar
- Zest of 2 lemons
- 1/2 cup lemon curd

Instructions

1. In a bowl, mix the heavy cream, whole milk, and granulated sugar. Whip the sugar until completely dissolved.

2. Add the zest of two lemons to the mixture, infusing it with fresh citrus flavor.

3. Incorporate the lemon curd into the mixture, stirring until it's evenly distributed. The lemon curd will add both tanginess and sweetness to the ice cream.

4. Transfer the lemon-infused mixture to a CREAMi Pint, seal it with the storage lid, and place it in the freezer for a minimum of 4 hours. This allows the ice cream to set and develop its delightful consistency.

5. After the freezing time, remove the CREAMi Pint out of the freezer, then take off the lid. Put the CREAMi pint in the outer bowl. Ensure the Creamerizer Paddle is attached to the outer bowl lid, and lock the lid assembly onto the outer bowl.

6. Position the bowl onto the base and turn the handle towards the right in order to secure it. Select the Ice Cream function to begin churning.

7. As soon as the churning process is completed, your Lemon Curd Ice Cream is ready to be enjoyed. It's a delightful blend of citrusy zest and creaminess. Serve it immediately for the freshest taste.

PREP TIP:

For an extra burst of lemon flavor, you can add a squeeze of fresh lemon juice before serving.

Mocha Almond Fudge Ice Cream

SERVES 4

Indulge in the best of both worlds with Mocha Almond Fudge Ice Cream. This delectable treat combines the robust flavors of coffee and chocolate with the satisfying crunch of almonds and the richness of fudge. It's an irresistible dessert for coffee and chocolate lovers alike.

PREP TIME: 10 minutes / Freeze time: 4 hours

FUNCTION: Ice Cream

TOOLS NEEDED: Mixing bowl, whisk or rubber spatula

Ingredients

- 2 cups of heavy cream
- 1 cup of whole milk
- 3/4 cup of granulated sugar
- 2 tablespoons unsweetened cocoa powder
- 2 tablespoons instant coffee granules
- 1/2 cup chopped almonds (toasted)
- 1/2 cup fudge sauce

Instructions

1. Combine in a mixing bowl the heavy cream, granulated sugar, whole milk, unsweetened cocoa powder, and instant coffee granules. Whip the sugar until completely dissolved, and the cocoa and coffee are well incorporated into the mixture.

2. Fold in the toasted chopped almonds, ensuring they are evenly distributed throughout the mixture.

3. Transfer the mocha almond fudge ice cream base to a CREAMi Pint. Seal the container with the storage lid and place it in the freezer for a minimum of 4 hours. This resting period allows the flavors to meld and the ice cream to achieve the desired creamy texture.

4. After the freezing time, remove the CREAMi Pint out of the freezer, then take off the lid. Put the CREAMi pint in the outer bowl. Ensure that the Creamerizer Paddle is attached to the outer bowl lid, and lock the lid assembly onto the outer bowl.

5. Position the bowl components on the motor-base and secure by turning the handle to the right. Select the Ice Cream function to initiate the churning process.

6. Once the machine has completed churning, your Mocha Almond Fudge Ice Cream is ready to be savored. Serve it immediately, drizzling each serving with a generous amount of fudge sauce for that extra indulgence.

PREP TIP:

Toasting the almonds in a dry skillet for a few minutes enhances their flavor and provides a delightful crunch.

Blueberry Cheesecake Ice Cream

SERVES 4

Blueberry Cheesecake Ice Cream is the perfect marriage of creamy indulgence and fruity delight. This dessert captures the essence of a classic cheesecake with a swirl of vibrant blueberry compote, all nestled within a velvety ice cream base.

PREP TIME: 20 minutes / Freeze time: 4 hours

FUNCTION: Ice Cream

TOOLS NEEDED: Mixing bowl, whisk or rubber spatula, saucepan

Ingredients

For the Blueberry Compote:

- 1 cup fresh or frozen blueberries
- 1/4 cup granulated sugar
- 1 tablespoon lemon juice

For the Cheesecake Base:

- 2 cups of heavy cream
- 1 cup of whole milk
- 3/4 cup of granulated sugar
- 4 ounces cream cheese, softened
- 1 teaspoon pure vanilla extract

Instructions

For the Blueberry Compote:

1. In a saucepan, combine the blueberries, granulated sugar, and lemon juice. Heat the mixture over medium-low heat, stirring occasionally, until the blueberries break down and the sauce thickens, about 10 minutes. Remove it from the heat and let it cool completely.

For the Cheesecake Base:

1. In a mixing bowl, whisk together the heavy cream, whole milk, and granulated sugar until the sugar is fully dissolved.

2. In a separate bowl, soften the cream cheese by microwaving it for 10-15 seconds until it's easy to work with.

3. Add the softened cream cheese and pure vanilla extract to the cream mixture. Whisk until all the ingredients are well combined, and the mixture is smooth.

Assembling the Ice Cream:

1. Pour half of the cheesecake base into a CREAMi Pint and seal it with the storage lid.

2. Spoon half of the blueberry compote over the cheesecake base.

3. Repeat the layers with the remaining cheesecake base and blueberry compote.

4. Use a knife or spatula to gently swirl the layers together, creating a marbled effect.

5. Freeze the pint for a minimum of 4 hours to allow the flavors to meld and the ice cream to set.

6. When ready to serve, remove the CREAMi Pint from the freezer, take off the lid, and scoop out the Blueberry Cheesecake Ice Cream into bowls or cones. Enjoy this delectable dessert that combines the best of cheesecake and ice cream in every bite.

PREP TIP:

For the best results, make sure the blueberry compote is fully cooled before layering it with the cheesecake base.

Philadelphia-Style Chocolate Ice Cream

SERVES 4

Indulge in the rich, velvety goodness of Philadelphia-Style Chocolate Ice Cream. This egg-free recipe captures the essence of chocolate in every creamy spoonful. It's pure chocolatey bliss!

PREP TIME: 15 minutes / Freeze time: 4 hours

FUNCTION: Ice Cream

TOOLS NEEDED: Mixing bowl, whisk or rubber spatula

Ingredients

- 2 cups of heavy cream
- 1 cup of whole milk
- 1 cup granulated sugar
- 1/2 cup unsweetened cocoa powder
- 1/4 cup chocolate fudge sauce

Instructions

1. Combine in a mixing bowl the heavy cream, granulated sugar, whole milk , and unsweetened cocoa powder. Whip the sugar until completely dissolved.

2. Gently blend in the chocolate fudge sauce, ensuring it's evenly distributed throughout the mixture.

3. Transfer the chocolatey base to a CREAMi Pint and secure the lid. Freeze for at least 4 hours, allowing the flavors to meld and the ice cream to attain its signature creamy texture.

4. After the freezing period, take the CREAMi Pint out and remove the lid. Put the CREAMi pint in the outer bowl, ensuring the Creamerizer Paddle is attached onto the lid of the outer bowl, and lock.

5. Position the bowl onto the base and turn the handle towards the right in order to secure it. Select the Ice Cream function to initiate the churning process.

6. Once the churning process is complete, your Philadelphia-Style Chocolate Ice Cream is ready to be savored. Serve it immediately for a delightful chocolatey experience.

PREP TIP:

For an even more intense chocolate flavor, consider using high-quality cocoa powder.

Gelatos

Traditional Italian Gelato

SERVES 4

Indulge in the exquisite taste of Traditional Italian Gelato, a dessert that embodies the artistry and passion of Italian culinary tradition. This recipe captures the essence of Italy's gelato, known for its smooth, dense, and intensely flavorful texture.

PREP TIME: 20 minutes / Freeze time: 4-6 hours

FUNCTION: Gelato

TOOLS NEEDED: Ice cream maker, mixing bowl, whisk

Ingredients

- 2 cups whole milk
- 1 cup heavy cream
- 3/4 cup of granulated sugar
- 4 large egg yolks
- 1 vanilla bean, split and seeds scraped
- 1/2 cup fresh fruit puree (e.g., strawberry, raspberry, or mango)

Instructions

1. Begin by combining the whole milk and heavy cream in a mixing bowl. Heat the mixture over medium-low heat in a saucepan until it begins to steam. Avoid boiling it.

2. While the milk and cream mixture is warming, whisk together the granulated sugar and egg yolks in a separate bowl until they become pale and slightly thickened.

3. Once the milk mixture is steaming, remove it from the heat and slowly pour it into the egg yolk mixture, whisking continuously to prevent curdling.

4. Return the combined mixture to the saucepan and place it over low heat. Stir constantly with a wooden spoon until the mixture thickens and coats the back of the spoon. This is known as "tempering" the mixture and should take about 5-7 minutes.

5. Remove the mixture from the heat and stir in the scraped seeds from the vanilla bean. Allow it to cool to room temperature.

6. Once cooled, cover the mixture and refrigerate it for at least 2 hours or until it's thoroughly chilled.

7. When ready to make the gelato, pour the chilled mixture into your ice cream maker and churn according to the manufacturer's instructions. This usually takes 20-25 minutes.

8. During the last 5 minutes of churning, add the fresh fruit puree to the gelato and continue churning until it's fully incorporated.

9. Transfer the churned gelato to an airtight container and freeze for an additional 2-4 hours to achieve the perfect gelato texture.

10. Serve your Traditional Italian Gelato in small scoops or elegant quenelles. Garnish with fresh fruit or a sprig of mint for an authentic Italian touch.

PREP TIP:

For a velvety-smooth gelato, ensure that the mixture is well-chilled before churning, and don't rush the freezing process.

Hazelnut Gelato

SERVES 4

Indulge in the delightful nuttiness of Hazelnut Gelato. With its rich hazelnut flavor, this creamy Italian treat is a perfect balance of sweet and nutty notes. It's a delightful variation of traditional gelato that's sure to please your taste buds.

PREP TIME: 15 minutes / Freeze time: 4 hours

FUNCTION: Gelato

TOOLS NEEDED: Mixing bowl, whisk or rubber spatula

Ingredients

- 1 cup hazelnuts
- 2 cups whole milk
- 1 cup heavy cream
- 3/4 cup of granulated sugar
- 1 teaspoon pure vanilla extract
- A pinch of salt

Instructions

1. Begin by toasting the hazelnuts to enhance their flavor. Preheat your oven to 350°F (175°C). Spread the hazelnuts evenly on a baking sheet and toast them in the oven for about 10-12 minutes or until they become fragrant. Remove them from the oven and allow them to cool. Once cooled, rub the hazelnuts with a kitchen towel to remove their skins.

2. In a blender or food processor, grind the toasted and peeled hazelnuts into a fine powder. Set this hazelnut powder aside for later use.

3. In a mixing bowl, combine the whole milk, heavy cream, granulated sugar, pure vanilla extract, and a pinch of salt. Whip the sugar until completely dissolved.

4. Add the ground hazelnut powder to the mixture and whisk until it is thoroughly incorporated.

5. Transfer the hazelnut-infused mixture to a CREAMi Pint, seal it with the storage lid, and place it in the freezer for a minimum of 4 hours. This chilling period is essential for achieving the desired creamy texture.

6. After the freezing time, take the CREAMi Pint out and remove the lid. Put the CREAMi pint in the outer bowl, ensuring the Creamerizer Paddle is attached onto the lid of the outer bowl, and lock.

7. Position the bowl onto the base and turn the handle towards the right in order to secure it. Select the Gelato function to begin churning.

8. As soon as the churning process is completed, your Hazelnut Gelato is ready to be enjoyed. Serve it immediately, savoring the rich hazelnut flavor.

PREP TIP:

To enhance the hazelnut flavor, you can add a drizzle of hazelnut syrup or a sprinkle of chopped hazelnuts as a topping.

Lemon Basil Gelato

SERVES 4

Lemon Basil Gelato is a delightful fusion of citrusy brightness and the aromatic essence of basil. This refreshing treat captures the essence of summer in a frozen dessert, offering a burst of tangy and herbal flavors that dance on your taste buds.

PREP TIME: 15 minutes / Freeze time: 4 hours

FUNCTION: Gelato

TOOLS NEEDED: Saucepan, whisk, mixing bowl

Ingredients

- 2 cups whole milk
- 1 cup heavy cream
- 1 cup granulated sugar
- Zest of 2 lemons
- 1/4 cup fresh lemon juice
- 1/4 cup fresh basil leaves, chopped

Instructions

1. Start by preparing the base. In a saucepan, combine the whole milk and heavy cream. Place it over medium heat and warm the mixture until it's just about to simmer. Do not bring it to a boil.

2. In a mixing bowl, whisk together the granulated sugar and the lemon zest. Whisk until the sugar becomes infused with the bright lemon aroma.

3. Gradually pour the warm milk and cream mixture into the bowl with the sugar and lemon zest. Stir until the sugar is completely dissolved.

4. Once the mixture is well combined, add the fresh lemon juice and the chopped fresh basil leaves. Stir again to incorporate these delightful flavors.

5. Allow the mixture to cool to room temperature. Once it has cooled, cover the bowl and refrigerate it for at least 2 hours. Chilling the mixture thoroughly is crucial to ensure a creamy gelato.

6. After the mixture has chilled, transfer it to your gelato maker and churn according to the manufacturer's instructions. This typically takes about 20-25 minutes.

7. Once the gelato reaches a creamy, frozen consistency, transfer it to an airtight container and freeze for an additional 2 hours to firm up.

8. When you're ready to serve, scoop the Lemon Basil Gelato into bowls or cones, garnishing with a sprig of fresh basil or a twist of lemon zest for an extra touch of elegance.

PREP TIP:

For a more pronounced basil flavor, steep the basil leaves in the warm milk and cream mixture for 15-20 minutes before straining them out.

Espresso Gelato

SERVES 4

Espresso Gelato is a coffee lover's dream dessert. It combines the bold and rich flavors of espresso with the creamy, smooth texture of gelato. This indulgent treat is perfect for those who appreciate the bittersweet allure of coffee in their desserts.

PREP TIME: 15 minutes / Freeze time: 4 hours

FUNCTION: Gelato

TOOLS NEEDED: Mixing bowl, whisk, espresso machine or strong brewed coffee maker

Ingredients

- 2 cups of heavy cream
- 1 cup of whole milk
- 3/4 cup of granulated sugar
- 1/2 cup strong brewed espresso (cooled)
- 1 teaspoon pure vanilla extract

Instructions

1. Start by brewing a strong cup of espresso and allowing it to cool. Alternatively, use a strong brewed coffee.

2. In a bowl, mix the heavy cream, whole milk, and granulated sugar. Whip the sugar until completely dissolved.

3. Add the cooled espresso and pure vanilla extract to the mixture. Stir until well combined, ensuring that the coffee flavor is evenly distributed.

4. Transfer the mixture to a CREAMi Pint, seal it with the storage lid, and place it in the freezer for a minimum of 4 hours. This freezing time allows the gelato to achieve its creamy consistency while preserving the coffee flavor.

5. After the freezing period, take the CREAMi Pint out and remove the lid. Put the CREAMi pint in the outer bowl, ensuring that the Creamerizer Paddle is attached onto the lid of the outer bowl, and lock.

6. Position the bowl components on the motor-base and secure by turning the handle to the right. Select the Gelato function to begin churning.

7. As soon as the churning process is completed, your Espresso Gelato is ready to be enjoyed. Serve it immediately in small scoops or as a refreshing affogato by pouring a shot of hot espresso over a scoop of gelato.

PREP TIP:

For a stronger coffee flavor, you can adjust the amount of espresso or brewed coffee to your taste preference.

Pistachio Gelato

SERVES 4

Pistachio Gelato is an exquisite Italian dessert known for its rich, nutty flavor and creamy texture. This recipe captures the essence of pistachios, creating a delightful treat that's perfect for any occasion.

PREP TIME: 15 minutes / Freeze time: 4 hours

FUNCTION: Gelato

TOOLS NEEDED: Food processor or blender, mixing bowl, whisk or rubber spatula

Ingredients

- 1 cup unsalted pistachios, shelled and roasted
- 2 cups whole milk
- 3/4 cup of granulated sugar
- 1/2 teaspoon almond extract
- A pinch of salt
- 1/4 cup heavy cream

Instructions

1. Begin by preparing the pistachios. Shell and roast them if they're not already roasted. Once roasted, allow them to cool completely.

2. In a food processor or blender, pulse the pistachios until finely ground. You want a texture that's not quite a powder but not too coarse either; a fine crumb texture is ideal.

3. In a mixing bowl, combine the ground pistachios, granulated sugar, almond extract, and a pinch of salt. Mix these dry ingredients until well combined.

4. Slowly pour in the whole milk while whisking. Continue to whisk until the mixture is smooth and the sugar is fully dissolved.

5. Add the heavy cream to the mixture and whisk until everything is thoroughly combined.

6. Transfer the pistachio mixture to a gelato maker or ice cream maker according to the manufacturer's instructions. Typically, this involves churning the mixture for about 20-25 minutes until it reaches a creamy, gelato-like consistency.

7. Once the gelato is ready, transfer it to an airtight container and freeze it for at least 4 hours or until firm.

8. When serving, let the gelato sit at room temperature for a few minutes to soften slightly for the best texture. Scoop and enjoy the delightful nuttiness of Pistachio Gelato.

PREP TIP:

For added texture, consider reserving a handful of chopped pistachios to fold into the gelato before freezing.

Dark Chocolate Gelato

SERVES 4

Indulge in the deep, velvety decadence of Dark Chocolate Gelato. This recipe elevates the classic Italian dessert to new heights with its intense cocoa flavor and irresistibly smooth texture.

PREP TIME: 15 minutes / Freeze time: 4 hours

FUNCTION: Gelato

TOOLS NEEDED: Mixing bowl, whisk or rubber spatula

Ingredients

- 2 cups whole milk
- 1 cup heavy cream
- 3/4 cup of granulated sugar
- 1/2 cup unsweetened cocoa powder
- 4 ounces dark chocolate (70% cocoa or higher), finely chopped
- 1 teaspoon pure vanilla extract
- A pinch of salt

Instructions

1. In a mixing bowl, combine the whole milk and heavy cream. Stir until well mixed.

2. In a separate bowl, sift the unsweetened cocoa powder to remove any lumps. Add the sifted cocoa powder to the milk and cream mixture. Whisk until the cocoa powder is fully dissolved.

3. In a microwave-safe bowl, melt the finely chopped dark chocolate in 20-second intervals, stirring between each interval until it's completely smooth. Allow it to cool slightly.

4. Add the melted dark chocolate, granulated sugar, pure vanilla extract, and a pinch of salt to the milk and cream mixture. Stir until all the ingredients are thoroughly combined.

5. Transfer the mixture to a CREAMi Pint, seal it with the storage lid, and place it in the freezer for at least 4 hours. This freezing time is essential for achieving the gelato's perfect consistency.

6. Once the gelato base has thoroughly chilled, remove the CREAMi Pint out of the freezer, then take off the lid. Put the CREAMi pint in the outer bowl. Ensure the Creamerizer Paddle is attached to the lid of the outer bowl and lock the assembly into place.

7. Position the bowl onto the base and turn the handle towards the right in order to secure it. Select the Gelato function to begin churning.

8. When the machine has finished churning, your Dark Chocolate Gelato is ready to enjoy. Serve it immediately in chilled bowls or cones for a truly indulgent treat.

PREP TIP:

For added richness and depth, choose high-quality dark chocolate with at least 70% cocoa content.

Amaretto Gelato

SERVES 4

Amaretto Gelato is a luxurious Italian dessert that captivates with its rich almond flavor and silky-smooth texture. This recipe brings the essence of Italy right to your kitchen, and it's surprisingly simple to make.

PREP TIME: 10 minutes / Freeze time: 4 hours

FUNCTION: Gelato

TOOLS NEEDED: Mixing bowl, whisk or rubber spatula

Ingredients

- 2 cups whole milk
- 1 cup heavy cream
- 3/4 cup of granulated sugar
- 1/2 cup amaretto liqueur
- 1 teaspoon almond extract
- 1/2 cup finely chopped toasted almonds

Instructions

1. In a mixing bowl, combine the whole milk, heavy cream, and granulated sugar. Whip the sugar until completely dissolved.

2. Add the amaretto liqueur and almond extract to the mixture. Stir until well combined.

3. Transfer the mixture to your ice cream maker's gelato setting or a CREAMi Pint if using a Ninja CREAMi. If using the CREAMi Pint, seal it with the

storage lid and place it in the freezer for a minimum of 4 hours. Gelato should have a slightly softer consistency than ice cream.

4. If using an ice cream maker, follow the manufacturer's instructions to churn the mixture into gelato.

5. If using the Ninja CREAMi, after the freezing time, take the CREAMi Pint out and remove the lid. Put the CREAMi pint in the outer bowl, ensuring the Creamerizer Paddle is attached onto the lid of the outer bowl, and lock.

6. Position the bowl onto the base and turn the handle towards the right in order to secure it. Select the Gelato function to churn the mixture into a creamy gelato.

7. Once the churning process is complete, fold in the finely chopped toasted almonds to add a delightful crunch to your Amaretto Gelato.

8. Your homemade Amaretto Gelato is now ready to be enjoyed. Serve it in small scoops in chilled bowls or cones for an authentic Italian experience.

PREP TIP:

For the best flavor, use high-quality amaretto liqueur and toasted almonds.

Caramel Macchiato Gelato

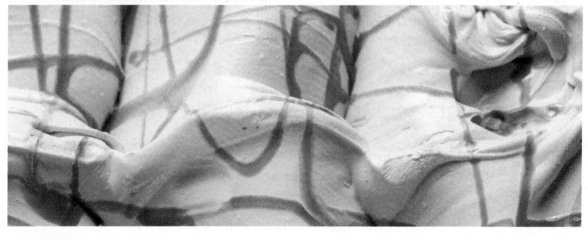

SERVES 4

Indulge in the irresistible fusion of rich caramel and bold espresso with Caramel Macchiato Gelato. This luscious dessert offers the perfect balance of sweetness and coffee bitterness, making it a delightful treat for coffee lovers.

PREP TIME: 20 minutes / Freeze time: 4 hours

FUNCTION: Gelato

TOOLS NEEDED: Mixing bowl, whisk or rubber spatula

Ingredients

- 2 cups whole milk
- 1 cup heavy cream
- 3/4 cup of granulated sugar
- 2 tablespoons instant espresso powder
- 1/4 cup caramel sauce, plus extra for drizzling
- 1 teaspoon pure vanilla extract

Instructions

1. In a mixing bowl, combine the whole milk, heavy cream, and granulated sugar. Whip the sugar until completely dissolved.

2. Add the instant espresso powder to the mixture and whisk vigorously until the espresso is completely dissolved, and the mixture takes on a rich coffee flavor.

3. Stir in the caramel sauce and pure vanilla extract until everything is well incorporated.

4. Transfer the mixture to a CREAMi Pint, seal it with the storage lid, and place it in the freezer for a minimum of 4 hours. This chilling time allows the flavors to meld and the gelato to achieve the desired texture.

5. After the freezing period, remove the CREAMi Pint out of the freezer, then take off the lid. Put the CREAMi pint in the outer bowl. Ensure the Creamerizer Paddle is attached to the outer bowl lid, and lock the lid assembly onto the outer bowl.

6. Position the bowl onto the base and turn the handle towards the right in order to secure it. Select the Gelato function to begin churning.

7. While the gelato is churning, periodically drizzle additional caramel sauce into the mixture to create ribbons of caramel throughout.

8. As soon as the churning process is completed, your Caramel Macchiato Gelato is ready to be savored. Serve it immediately, drizzled with extra caramel sauce if desired.

PREP TIP:

For an even stronger coffee flavor, you can increase the amount of instant espresso powder.

Fig and Walnut Gelato

SERVES 4

Indulge in the delightful harmony of sweet figs and crunchy walnuts with this Fig and Walnut Gelato. The richness of the figs blends seamlessly with the earthy notes of walnuts, creating a balanced and satisfying frozen treat.

PREP TIME: 20 minutes / Freeze time: 4 hours

FUNCTION: Gelato

TOOLS NEEDED: Mixing bowl, whisk, ice cream maker

Ingredients

- 1 cup fresh figs, stems removed and chopped
- 1/2 cup chopped walnuts
- 2/3 cup granulated sugar
- 1 1/2 cups whole milk
- 1 1/2 cups of heavy cream
- 1 teaspoon pure vanilla extract

Instructions

1. Begin by preparing the figs. Remove the stems and chop them into small pieces. Set them aside.

2. In a mixing bowl, combine the chopped figs and walnuts. Add 1/3 cup of granulated sugar to this mixture and stir until the sugar coats the figs and

walnuts evenly. Let this mixture sit for about 15 minutes to allow the figs to release their juices.

3. After the fig mixture has macerated, use a fork to mash the figs slightly, creating a coarse paste with some small chunks.

4. In a separate bowl, whisk together the remaining 1/3 cup of granulated sugar, whole milk, heavy cream, and pure vanilla extract until the sugar is fully dissolved.

5. Combine the fig and walnut mixture with the milk and cream mixture, stirring until everything is well incorporated.

6. Pour the combined mixture into your ice cream maker and churn according to the manufacturer's instructions. This typically takes about 20-25 minutes until the gelato reaches a soft-serve consistency.

7. Transfer the freshly churned gelato into a lidded container and freeze it for at least 4 hours to firm up.

8. When serving, garnish your Fig and Walnut Gelato with a few chopped walnuts or fresh fig slices for added texture and presentation.

PREP TIP:

If fresh figs are unavailable, you can use dried figs that have been soaked in warm water until soft and then chopped.

Strawberry Balsamic Gelato

SERVES 4

Strawberry Balsamic Gelato is a sophisticated twist on a classic favorite. The sweetness of ripe strawberries is beautifully balanced by the subtle tang of balsamic vinegar, resulting in a harmonious and delightful dessert.

PREP TIME: 20 minutes / Freeze time: 4 hours

FUNCTION: Gelato

TOOLS NEEDED: Blender, mixing bowl, whisk or rubber spatula

Ingredients

- 2 cups fresh strawberries, hulled and halved
- 1 tablespoon balsamic vinegar
- 1 cup of whole milk
- 3/4 cup of granulated sugar
- 1 teaspoon pure vanilla extract
- 1/2 cup heavy (whipping) cream

Instructions

1. Start by preparing the strawberries. Hull them and then halve them. Place the strawberries in a blender.

2. Add the balsamic vinegar to the strawberries in the blender. Blend until you have a smooth and vibrant strawberry puree.

3. In a mixing bowl, combine the whole milk, granulated sugar, and pure vanilla extract. Whip the sugar until completely dissolved.

4. Add the strawberry-balsamic puree to the milk mixture. Stir until everything is well combined.

5. Pour the gelato base into a CREAMi Pint, seal it with the storage lid, and place it in the freezer for a minimum of 4 hours. This will allow the flavors to meld, resulting in a delightful gelato texture.

6. After the freezing period, take the CREAMi Pint out and remove the lid. Put the CREAMi pint in the outer bowl. Ensure the Creamerizer Paddle is attached to the outer bowl lid, and lock the lid assembly onto the outer bowl.

7. Position the bowl onto the base and turn the handle towards the right in order to secure it. Select the Gelato function to begin churning.

8. Once the churning process is complete, your Strawberry Balsamic Gelato is ready to be savored. Serve it immediately, or for a firmer texture, transfer it to an airtight container and freeze for an additional hour before serving.

PREP TIP:

For a more intense balsamic flavor, you can drizzle a small amount of balsamic reduction over each serving before enjoying.

Ricotta and Pear Gelato

SERVES 4

Ricotta and Pear Gelato is a harmonious blend of creamy richness and the natural sweetness of ripe pears. This delightful frozen treat is a delightful departure from traditional gelato flavors, offering a unique and indulgent experience.

PREP TIME: 15 minutes / Freeze time: 4 hours

FUNCTION: Gelato

TOOLS NEEDED: Mixing bowl, whisk or rubber spatula

Ingredients

- 1 1/2 cups ripe pears, peeled, cored, and diced
- 2 tablespoons fresh lemon juice
- 1 cup of whole milk ricotta cheese
- 1/2 cup granulated sugar
- 1/2 cup heavy (whipping) cream
- 1/2 teaspoon pure vanilla extract

- A pinch of salt

Instructions

1. Begin by preparing the ripe pears. Peel, core, and dice them until you have about 1 1/2 cups of pear pieces.

2. In a mixing bowl, drizzle the fresh lemon juice over the diced pears. Toss them gently to coat. The lemon juice not only adds a zesty freshness but also prevents the pears from browning.

3. Using a blender or food processor, puree the lemon-coated pear pieces until you achieve a smooth consistency. Set this pear puree aside.

4. In a separate mixing bowl, combine the whole milk ricotta cheese, granulated sugar, heavy cream, pure vanilla extract, and a pinch of salt. Stir until all the ingredients are thoroughly blended.

5. Gradually incorporate the pear puree into the ricotta mixture, stirring gently until the two are fully combined. The result should be a smooth and creamy mixture with the pear's natural sweetness and the richness of ricotta.

6. Transfer the mixture to a clean CREAMi Pint, seal it with the storage lid, and place it in the freezer for a minimum of 4 hours. This chilling time is essential to achieve the desired gelato consistency.

7. After the freezing period, take the CREAMi Pint out and remove the lid. Put the CREAMi pint in the outer bowl, ensuring the Creamerizer Paddle is attached onto the lid of the outer bowl, and lock.

8. Position the bowl onto the base and turn the handle towards the right in order to secure it. Select the Gelato function to begin churning.

9. Once the machine completes the churning process, your Ricotta and Pear Gelato is ready to be savored. Serve it immediately to enjoy its creamy, fruity goodness.

PREP TIP:

Choose ripe pears for the best natural sweetness and flavor in your gelato.

Rosemary and Orange Gelato

SERVES 4

Indulge in the harmonious blend of aromatic rosemary and zesty orange in this exquisite Rosemary and Orange Gelato. It's a unique flavor combination that's both refreshing and sophisticated, making it a perfect treat for special occasions or simply when you want to elevate your dessert experience.

PREP TIME: 15 minutes / Freeze time: 4 hours

FUNCTION: Gelato

TOOLS NEEDED: Saucepan, whisk, mixing bowl

Ingredients

- 2 cups whole milk
- 1 cup heavy cream
- 3/4 cup of granulated sugar
- 2 sprigs fresh rosemary
- Zest of 2 oranges
- 4 large egg yolks
- 1 teaspoon pure vanilla extract
- 1/4 cup fresh orange juice

Instructions

1. In a saucepan, combine the whole milk, heavy cream, and half of the granulated sugar (approximately 3/8 cup). Place the saucepan over

medium heat and stir until the mixture is warm and the sugar has completely dissolved. Be careful not to let it boil.

2. While the milk and cream mixture is heating, add the fresh rosemary sprigs to infuse their flavor. Once the mixture is warm, remove it from the heat and let the rosemary steep for about 15 minutes. Then, strain out the rosemary and discard it.

3. In a mixing bowl, whisk together the remaining sugar and the egg yolks until the mixture is pale and slightly thickened.

4. Gradually pour the warm milk mixture into the egg yolk mixture, whisking constantly to prevent the eggs from curdling.

5. Return the combined mixture to the saucepan and place it over low heat. Cook, stirring constantly, until the mixture thickens and coats the back of a spoon. This usually takes about 5-7 minutes.

6. Remove the saucepan from the heat and stir in the orange zest, pure vanilla extract, and fresh orange juice. Mix well to incorporate all the flavors.

7. Let the mixture cool to room temperature, then cover it and refrigerate for at least 2 hours or until it's thoroughly chilled.

8. Once chilled, transfer the mixture to your gelato maker and churn according to the manufacturer's instructions.

9. When the gelato reaches a creamy consistency, transfer it to a lidded container and freeze for an additional 2-4 hours to firm up.

10. Serve your Rosemary and Orange Gelato in scoops, garnished with a sprig of fresh rosemary or a twist of orange zest for an extra touch of elegance.

PREP TIP:

Ensure that the rosemary is fresh and fragrant for the best flavor infusion.

Blackberry Cabernet Gelato

SERVES 4

Indulge in the rich and sophisticated flavors of Blackberry Cabernet Gelato. This luscious dessert combines the sweet and tart notes of blackberries with the subtle sophistication of Cabernet wine, resulting in a luxurious treat that's perfect for any occasion.

PREP TIME: 20 minutes / Freeze time: 4 hours

FUNCTION: Gelato

TOOLS NEEDED: Saucepan, fine-mesh strainer, mixing bowl, whisk

Ingredients

- 2 cups fresh blackberries
- 1/2 cup granulated sugar
- 1 cup of whole milk
- 1/2 cup heavy cream
- 1/2 cup Cabernet Sauvignon wine
- 1 teaspoon lemon zest
- 2 tablespoons lemon juice

Instructions

1. Begin by preparing the blackberry puree. In a saucepan over medium heat, combine the fresh blackberries and granulated sugar. Cook for about 5-7 minutes, or until the blackberries soften and release their juices. Use a fork or a potato masher to help break down the blackberries as they cook.

2. Once the blackberries have cooked down, remove the saucepan from the heat. Pass the mixture through a fine-mesh strainer into a mixing bowl, pressing down to extract as much liquid and pulp as possible. Discard the seeds and solids.

3. Add the whole milk, heavy cream, Cabernet Sauvignon wine, lemon zest, and lemon juice to the blackberry puree in the mixing bowl. Whisk until all the ingredients are thoroughly combined.

4. Cover the mixing bowl and refrigerate the mixture for at least 2 hours to chill it thoroughly.

5. After the mixture has chilled, pour it into your gelato maker and churn according to the manufacturer's instructions. Typically, this will take about 20-25 minutes.

6. Once the gelato has reached the desired consistency, transfer it to an airtight container and freeze for at least 2 hours to firm up.

7. Serve your homemade Blackberry Cabernet Gelato in bowls or cones and savor the delightful combination of sweet blackberries and the subtle richness of Cabernet wine.

PREP TIP:

For the best flavor, use a high-quality Cabernet Sauvignon wine.

Toasted Almond Gelato

SERVES 4

Indulge in the rich and nutty delight of Toasted Almond Gelato, a frozen treat that's sure to captivate your taste buds. This recipe is designed for use with the Ninja CREAMi, ensuring a creamy and satisfying outcome.

PREP TIME: 15 minutes / Freeze time: 4 hours

FUNCTION: Gelato

TOOLS NEEDED: Mixing bowl, whisk or rubber spatula

Ingredients

- 2 cups of heavy cream

- 1 cup of whole milk

- 3/4 cup of granulated sugar

- 1 cup toasted almonds, chopped

- 1 teaspoon almond extract

- 1/2 teaspoon pure vanilla extract

Instructions

1. Begin by toasting the almonds. In a dry skillet over medium heat, add the chopped almonds. Toast them, stirring frequently, until they become fragrant and lightly golden, usually around 5 minutes. Be attentive to prevent burning. Once toasted, remove from heat and let them cool completely.

2. In a bowl, mix the heavy cream, whole milk, and granulated sugar. Stir until the sugar is completely dissolved.

3. Add the toasted almonds, almond extract, and pure vanilla extract to the mixture. Stir until well combined.

4. Transfer the mixture to a CREAMi Pint, seal it with the storage lid, and place it in the freezer for a minimum of 4 hours. This freezing time is crucial to achieve the desired gelato consistency.

5. After the freezing period, take the CREAMi Pint out and remove the lid. Put the CREAMi pint in the outer bowl, ensuring that the Creamerizer Paddle is attached onto the lid of the outer bowl, and lock.

6. Position the bowl onto the base and turn the handle towards the right in order to secure it. Select the Gelato function to begin churning.

7. As soon as the churning process is completed, your indulgent Toasted Almond Gelato is ready to be savored. Serve it immediately as a delightful dessert.

PREP TIP:

For extra nutty flavor, you can reserve a handful of toasted almonds to sprinkle on top of each serving.

Coconut Lime Gelato

SERVES 4

Indulge in the tropical fusion of flavors with Coconut Lime Gelato. This delightful frozen treat combines the creamy richness of coconut with the zesty freshness of lime, creating a refreshing dessert that's perfect for any occasion.

PREP TIME: 15 minutes / Freeze time: 4 hours

FUNCTION: Gelato

TOOLS NEEDED: Mixing bowl, whisk or rubber spatula

Ingredients

- 2 cups coconut milk
- 1 cup of whole milk
- 3/4 cup of granulated sugar
- Zest and juice of 3 limes
- 1/2 teaspoon pure vanilla extract

Instructions

1. In a mixing bowl, combine the coconut milk, whole milk, and granulated sugar. Whip the sugar until completely dissolved.

2. Add the zest and juice of three limes to the mixture. This will infuse the gelato with the vibrant, zesty flavor of lime. Stir until well combined.

3. Incorporate the pure vanilla extract into the mixture, enhancing the overall flavor profile.

4. Transfer the well-blended mixture to a CREAMi Pint, seal it with the storage lid, and place it in the freezer for a minimum of 4 hours. This resting period allows the flavors to meld and the gelato to achieve its delightful texture.

5. Once the freezing time has elapsed, remove the CREAMi Pint out of the freezer, then take off the lid. Put the CREAMi pint in the outer bowl. Ensure that the Creamerizer Paddle is securely attached to the outer bowl lid, and lock the lid assembly onto the outer bowl.

6. Position the bowl assembly on the motor base, and twist the handle to the right to raise the platform and lock it in place. Select the Gelato function to initiate the churning process.

7. After the churning is complete, your Coconut Lime Gelato is ready to be enjoyed. Serve it immediately as a refreshing and tropical dessert.

PREP TIP:

For an added touch of visual appeal, garnish your Coconut Lime Gelato with a sprinkle of fresh lime zest before serving.

Spiced Apple Gelato

SERVES 4

Indulge in the warm and comforting flavors of autumn with Spiced Apple Gelato. Made using the innovative Ninja CREAMi, this recipe transforms crisp apples and aromatic spices into a creamy, delightful frozen treat.

PREP TIME: 15 minutes / Freeze time: 4 hours

FUNCTION: Gelato

TOOLS NEEDED: Ninja CREAMi, large mixing bowl, whisk or rubber spatula

Ingredients

- 4 medium-sized apples, peeled, cored, and diced
- 1/2 cup granulated sugar
- 1 teaspoon ground cinnamon
- 1/2 teaspoon ground nutmeg
- 1/4 teaspoon ground cloves
- 1/2 teaspoon pure vanilla extract
- 1 cup heavy (whipping) cream
- 1/2 cup whole milk
- 1 tablespoon lemon juice

Instructions

1. Begin by preparing the spiced apple mixture. In a large mixing bowl, combine the diced apples, granulated sugar, ground cinnamon, ground nutmeg, and ground cloves. Toss the mixture until the apples are evenly coated in the spices and sugar. Let this mixture sit for about 10 minutes to allow the flavors to meld.

2. After the resting period, transfer the spiced apple mixture to a saucepan. Cook the mixture over medium heat, stirring occasionally, until the apples become soft and tender. This should take approximately 10-12 minutes.

3. Once the apples have softened, remove them from the heat and let them cool to room temperature.

4. Using a blender or food processor, puree the cooled spiced apple mixture until it becomes smooth and creamy. You can adjust the consistency by adding a bit of water if needed.

5. In a separate mixing bowl, combine the pureed spiced apple mixture with the pure vanilla extract, heavy cream, whole milk, and lemon juice. Stir until all the ingredients are well combined.

6. Transfer the gelato base to a CREAMi Pint, seal it with the storage lid, and place it in the freezer for a minimum of 4 hours. This freezing time is essential to achieve the desired gelato texture.

7. Once the gelato has sufficiently frozen, take the CREAMi Pint out and remove the lid. Put the CREAMi pint in the outer bowl. Ensure the Creamerizer Paddle is attached to the outer bowl lid, and lock the lid assembly onto the outer bowl.

8. Position the bowl onto the base and turn the handle towards the right in order to secure it. Select the Gelato function to begin the churning process.

9. After the Ninja CREAMi has completed churning, your Spiced Apple Gelato is ready to be enjoyed. Serve it immediately, savoring the delightful combination of apple and spices. Optionally, you can garnish it with a sprinkle of cinnamon or a drizzle of caramel sauce.

PREP TIP:

For a more pronounced spice flavor, you can adjust the amount of cinnamon, nutmeg, and cloves to suit your taste preferences.

White Chocolate Lavender Gelato

SERVES 4

Indulge in the luxurious and aromatic delight of White Chocolate Lavender Gelato. This exquisite frozen treat marries the creamy sweetness of white chocolate with the subtle floral notes of lavender, creating a dessert that's as elegant as it is delicious.

PREP TIME: 20 minutes / Freeze time: 4 hours

FUNCTION: Gelato

TOOLS NEEDED: Mixing bowl, whisk or rubber spatula

Ingredients

- 2 cups of heavy cream
- 1 cup of whole milk
- 3/4 cup of granulated sugar
- 1/2 cup high-quality white chocolate, finely chopped
- 2 tablespoons dried culinary lavender buds
- 1 teaspoon pure vanilla extract

Instructions

1. In a bowl, mix the heavy cream, whole milk, and granulated sugar. Stir until the sugar is completely dissolved.

2. In a separate microwave-safe bowl, place the finely chopped white chocolate. Microwave it in short 15-second intervals, stirring between each, until the chocolate is smooth and fully melted. Allow it to cool slightly.

3. Once the white chocolate is slightly cooled, add it to the cream mixture. Mix until the chocolate is fully incorporated.

4. Gently crush the dried culinary lavender buds between your fingers to release their aroma, and then add them to the mixture. Stir to evenly distribute the lavender.

5. Stir in the pure vanilla extract to complete the flavor profile.

6. Transfer the gelato base to a CREAMi Pint and seal it with the storage lid. Freeze for a minimum of 4 hours to achieve the perfect gelato consistency.

7. After the freezing period, take the CREAMi Pint out and remove the lid. Put the CREAMi pint in the outer bowl. Ensure that the Creamerizer Paddle is attached to the lid of the outer bowl and lock the assembly into place.

8. Position the bowl onto the base and turn the handle towards the right in order to secure it. Select the Gelato function to start the churning process.

9. Once the churning is complete, your White Chocolate Lavender Gelato is ready to be enjoyed. Serve it immediately in small, elegant bowls to savor the decadence of this floral-infused treat.

PREP TIP:

For an extra touch of elegance, garnish your White Chocolate Lavender Gelato with a few fresh lavender buds before serving.

Blood Orange Gelato

SERVES 4

Experience the vibrant and refreshing taste of Blood Orange Gelato. This dessert is a symphony of citrus flavors, with the bold and slightly tart notes of blood oranges beautifully complemented by the creamy richness of gelato.

PREP TIME: 20 minutes / Freeze time: 4 hours

FUNCTION: Gelato

TOOLS NEEDED: Mixing bowl, whisk or rubber spatula

Ingredients

- 2 cups of heavy cream
- 1 cup of whole milk
- 3/4 cup of granulated sugar
- 1 cup fresh blood orange juice (about 4-5 blood oranges)
- Zest of 2 blood oranges
- 1 teaspoon pure vanilla extract

Instructions

1. In a bowl, mix the heavy cream, whole milk, and granulated sugar. Whip the sugar until completely dissolved.

2. Juice the blood oranges to obtain 1 cup of fresh blood orange juice. Be sure to strain out any seeds or pulp.

3. Add the fresh blood orange juice and the zest of 2 blood oranges to the cream mixture. Stir well to incorporate the citrus flavors.

4. Finally, add the pure vanilla extract to the mixture and stir to complete the flavor profile.

5. Transfer the gelato base to a CREAMi Pint and seal it with the storage lid. Freeze for a minimum of 4 hours to achieve the ideal gelato texture.

6. After the freezing period, take the CREAMi Pint out and remove the lid. Put the CREAMi pint in the outer bowl. Ensure that the Creamerizer Paddle is attached to the lid of the outer bowl and lock the assembly into place.

7. Position the bowl onto the base and turn the handle towards the right in order to secure it. Select the Gelato function to initiate the churning process.

8. Once the churning is complete, your Blood Orange Gelato is ready to be savored. Serve it immediately to enjoy the bright and zesty flavors of this delightful dessert.

PREP TIP:

For an added burst of citrus aroma, consider garnishing your Blood Orange Gelato with a twist of fresh blood orange zest before serving.

Cardamom Gelato

SERVES 4

Cardamom Gelato offers a unique and exotic twist to traditional frozen desserts. The warm and aromatic notes of cardamom create a captivating flavor that's both comforting and indulgent.

PREP TIME: 15 minutes / Freeze time: 4 hours

FUNCTION: Gelato

TOOLS NEEDED: Mixing bowl, whisk or rubber spatula

Ingredients

- 2 cups of heavy cream
- 1 cup of whole milk
- 3/4 cup of granulated sugar
- 1 tablespoon ground cardamom
- 1 teaspoon pure vanilla extract
- 1/4 teaspoon ground cinnamon (optional)

Instructions

1. In a bowl, mix the heavy cream, whole milk, and granulated sugar. Stir until the sugar is completely dissolved.

2. Add the ground cardamom to the mixture. If you desire a subtle hint of cinnamon to complement the cardamom, add the ground cinnamon as well. Stir until the spices are well incorporated.

3. Finish the base by adding the pure vanilla extract. Mix until the flavors are evenly distributed.

4. Transfer the gelato base to a CREAMi Pint and seal it with the storage lid. Freeze for a minimum of 4 hours to allow the flavors to meld and the gelato to reach its ideal consistency.

5. After the freezing period, take the CREAMi Pint out and remove the lid. Put the CREAMi pint in the outer bowl. Make sure the Creamerizer Paddle is attached to the outer bowl lid, and lock the lid assembly onto the outer bowl.

6. Position the bowl assembly on the motor base, and twist the handle to the right to raise the platform and lock it in place. Select the Gelato function to commence the churning process.

7. Once the churning is complete, your Cardamom Gelato is ready to be savored. Serve it in elegant dishes to fully appreciate the exotic and aromatic flavor of this frozen delight.

PREP TIP:

For an extra burst of cardamom aroma, consider lightly toasting whole cardamom pods before grinding them into a fine powder.

Mango Chili Gelato

SERVES 4

Experience a tantalizing blend of sweet and spicy with Mango Chili Gelato. This unique frozen treat combines the tropical goodness of mangoes with a subtle kick of chili heat, creating a flavor sensation that's both refreshing and adventurous.

PREP TIME: 20 minutes / Freeze time: 4 hours

FUNCTION: Gelato

TOOLS NEEDED: Mixing bowl, whisk or rubber spatula

Ingredients

- 2 cups ripe mangoes, peeled, pitted, and diced (about 2 large mangoes)
- 1 cup heavy cream
- 1 cup of whole milk
- 3/4 cup of granulated sugar
- 1/2 teaspoon chili powder (adjust to taste)
- 1/2 teaspoon lime zest
- 1 teaspoon lime juice

Instructions

1. In a mixing bowl, combine the diced ripe mangoes, heavy cream, whole milk, and granulated sugar. Whip the sugar until completely dissolved.

2. Add the chili powder to the mixture. The amount you use will depend on your preference for heat. Start with 1/2 teaspoon and adjust to taste. Stir well to evenly distribute the chili powder.

3. Incorporate the lime zest and lime juice into the mixture. These citrusy notes will complement the sweetness and heat of the mango and chili.

4. Transfer the mango chili gelato base to a CREAMi Pint and seal it with the storage lid. Freeze for a minimum of 4 hours to achieve the perfect gelato consistency.

5. After the freezing period, take the CREAMi Pint out and remove the lid. Put the CREAMi pint in the outer bowl. Ensure that the Creamerizer Paddle is attached to the lid of the outer bowl and lock the assembly into place.

6. Position the bowl onto the base and turn the handle towards the right in order to secure it. Select the Gelato function to start the churning process.

7. Once the churning is complete, your Mango Chili Gelato is ready to be savored. Serve it immediately for a burst of sweet, spicy, and tangy flavors.

PREP TIP:

For an extra kick of heat, you can add a pinch of cayenne pepper to the mixture. Just be cautious, as chili heat can vary.

White Chocolate–Raspberry Gelato

SERVES 4

Indulge in the delightful fusion of creamy white chocolate and the tartness of ripe raspberries with this White Chocolate–Raspberry Gelato. It's an elegant frozen dessert that will leave your taste buds craving for more.

PREP TIME: 20 minutes / Freeze time: 4 hours

FUNCTION: Gelato

TOOLS NEEDED: Mixing bowl, whisk or rubber spatula

Ingredients

- 2 cups of heavy cream
- 1 cup of whole milk
- 1/2 cup granulated sugar
- 4 ounces white chocolate, finely chopped
- 1 cup fresh raspberries

Instructions

1. In a bowl, mix the heavy cream, whole milk, and granulated sugar. Whip the sugar until completely dissolved.

2. In a separate microwave-safe bowl, gently melt the finely chopped white chocolate in 20-second intervals until it's smooth and creamy. Be careful not to overheat.

3. Add the melted white chocolate to the cream mixture and stir until well combined.

4. Carefully fold in the fresh raspberries, allowing their vibrant red color and tartness to infuse into the mixture.

5. Transfer the combined mixture to a CREAMi Pint and secure the lid. Freeze for at least 4 hours to ensure the gelato attains its signature smooth texture.

6. After the freezing time, remove the CREAMi Pint out of the freezer, then take off the lid. Put the CREAMi pint in the outer bowl, ensuring the Creamerizer Paddle is attached onto the lid of the outer bowl, and lock.

7. Position the bowl onto the base and turn the handle towards the right in order to secure it. Select the Gelato function to start churning.

8. Once the churning process is complete, your White Chocolate–Raspberry Gelato is ready to be savored. Serve it immediately for the best taste experience.

PREP TIP:

For an extra touch of elegance, garnish with a few fresh raspberries and white chocolate shavings.

Strawberry Cheesecake Gelato

SERVES 4

Indulge in the creamy elegance of Strawberry Cheesecake Gelato. This delightful frozen dessert perfectly blends the richness of cheesecake with the sweet tang of fresh strawberries. It's a heavenly treat you won't be able to resist.

PREP TIME: 20 minutes / Freeze time: 4 hours

FUNCTION: Gelato

TOOLS NEEDED: Mixing bowl, whisk or rubber spatula

Ingredients

- 2 cups of heavy cream
- 1 cup of whole milk
- 3/4 cup of granulated sugar
- 8 ounces cream cheese, softened
- 1 cup fresh strawberries, hulled and pureed
- 1 teaspoon pure vanilla extract
- 1/2 cup graham cracker crumbs

Instructions

1. In a bowl, mix the heavy cream, whole milk, and granulated sugar. Whip the sugar until completely dissolved.

2. Add the softened cream cheese to the mixture. Using a whisk or rubber spatula, blend until the cream cheese is fully incorporated into the mixture, creating a smooth base.

3. Gently fold in the fresh strawberry puree, ensuring it's evenly distributed to infuse that delightful strawberry flavor.

4. Add the pure vanilla extract to the mixture and stir until well combined.

5. Transfer the mixture to a CREAMi Pint and secure the lid. Freeze for at least 4 hours to allow the gelato to achieve its creamy consistency.

6. After the freezing period, take the CREAMi Pint out and remove the lid. Put the CREAMi pint in the outer bowl, ensuring the Creamerizer Paddle is attached onto the lid of the outer bowl, and lock.

7. Position the bowl onto the base and turn the handle towards the right in order to secure it. Select the Gelato function to begin churning.

8. Once the churning process is complete, your Strawberry Cheesecake Gelato is ready to delight your taste buds. Serve it immediately, garnished with graham cracker crumbs for that authentic cheesecake touch.

PREP TIP:

For added texture and flavor, consider drizzling a thin ribbon of strawberry sauce on top before serving.

Red Velvet Gelato

SERVES 4

Indulge in the luxurious and velvety charm of Red Velvet Gelato. This dessert combines the elegance of red velvet cake with the creamy delight of gelato. It's a treat that's as visually stunning as it is delicious.

PREP TIME: 15 minutes / Freeze time: 4 hours

FUNCTION: Gelato

TOOLS NEEDED: Mixing bowl, whisk or rubber spatula

Ingredients

- 2 cups of heavy cream
- 1 cup of whole milk
- 3/4 cup of granulated sugar
- 2 tablespoons unsweetened cocoa powder
- 1 tablespoon red food coloring
- 1 teaspoon pure vanilla extract
- 1/2 cup red velvet cake crumbs (prepared)
- 1/4 cup white chocolate chips

Instructions

1. In a bowl, mix the heavy cream, whole milk, and granulated sugar. Whip the sugar until completely dissolved.

2. Add the unsweetened cocoa powder, red food coloring, and pure vanilla extract to the mixture. Stir until well combined, resulting in the iconic deep red hue of red velvet.

3. Gently fold in the red velvet cake crumbs and white chocolate chips to infuse the flavors and textures of red velvet cake into the gelato.

4. Transfer the mixture to a CREAMi Pint and secure the lid. Freeze for at least 4 hours, allowing the gelato to achieve its signature creamy texture while maintaining the rich red velvet flavor.

5. After the freezing period, retrieve the CREAMi Pint out of the freezer, then take off the lid. Put the CREAMi pint in the outer bowl, ensuring the Creamerizer Paddle is attached onto the lid of the outer bowl, and lock.

6. Position the bowl onto the base and turn the handle towards the right in order to secure it. Select the Gelato function to begin churning.

7. Once the churning process is complete, your Red Velvet Gelato is ready to enchant your taste buds. Serve it immediately, and revel in the delightful marriage of red velvet and creamy gelato.

PREP TIP:

For the red velvet cake crumbs, you can use leftover cake or prepare a small batch specifically for this recipe.

Tiramisu Gelato

SERVES 4

Indulge in the rich and sophisticated flavors of Italy with Tiramisu Gelato. This frozen delight captures the essence of the classic Italian dessert, delivering the perfect balance of coffee, mascarpone, and a hint of cocoa in every creamy spoonful.

PREP TIME: 20 minutes / Freeze time: 4 hours

FUNCTION: Gelato

TOOLS NEEDED: Mixing bowl, whisk or rubber spatula

Ingredients

- 2 cups of heavy cream
- 1 cup of whole milk
- 3/4 cup of granulated sugar
- 2 tablespoons instant espresso powder, dissolved in 2 tablespoons hot water
- 1/4 cup mascarpone cheese
- 1/4 cup unsweetened cocoa powder
- 1 teaspoon pure vanilla extract

Instructions

1. In a bowl, mix the heavy cream, whole milk, and granulated sugar. Whip the sugar until completely dissolved.

2. Dissolve the instant espresso powder in hot water, and add it to the mixture. Stir until well combined.

3. Gently fold in the mascarpone cheese to infuse the authentic Tiramisu flavor.

4. Add the unsweetened cocoa powder and pure vanilla extract to the mixture. Continue to stir until all ingredients are fully incorporated.

5. Transfer the mixture to a CREAMi Pint and secure the lid. Freeze for at least 4 hours to allow the flavors to meld and the gelato to achieve its signature creaminess.

6. After the freezing period, take the CREAMi Pint out and remove the lid. Put the CREAMi pint in the outer bowl, ensuring the Creamerizer Paddle is attached onto the lid of the outer bowl, and lock.

7. Position the bowl onto the base and turn the handle towards the right in order to secure it. Select the Gelato function to begin churning.

8. Once the churning process is complete, your Tiramisu Gelato is ready to transport you to the heart of Italy. Serve it immediately, and savor the authentic flavors of Tiramisu in a frozen form.

PREP TIP:

For an extra indulgent touch, garnish with a dusting of cocoa powder or a drizzle of espresso syrup before serving.

Chocolate-Hazelnut Gelato

SERVES 4

Indulge in the velvety richness of Chocolate-Hazelnut Gelato. This Italian-style frozen dessert combines the deep flavors of chocolate with the nutty goodness of hazelnuts, creating a truly decadent treat.

PREP TIME: 15 minutes / Freeze time: 4 hours

FUNCTION: Gelato

TOOLS NEEDED: Mixing bowl, whisk or rubber spatula

Ingredients

- 2 cups of heavy cream

- 1 cup of whole milk

- 3/4 cup of granulated sugar

- 1/2 cup chocolate hazelnut spread (e.g., Nutella)

- 1/2 cup chopped hazelnuts, toasted

Instructions

1. In a bowl, mix the heavy cream, whole milk, and granulated sugar. Whip the sugar until completely dissolved.

2. Add the chocolate hazelnut spread (such as Nutella) to the mixture. Stir vigorously until the spread is completely incorporated into the base, creating a smooth and luscious chocolate-hazelnut mixture.

3. Gently fold in the toasted chopped hazelnuts, infusing the gelato with a delightful nutty crunch.

4. Transfer the mixture to a CREAMi Pint and secure the lid. Freeze for a minimum of 4 hours, allowing the gelato to set to perfection.

5. After the freezing time, remove the CREAMi Pint out of the freezer, then take off the lid. Put the CREAMi pint in the outer bowl, ensuring the Creamerizer Paddle is attached onto the lid of the outer bowl, and lock.

6. Position the bowl onto the base and turn the handle towards the right in order to secure it. Select the Gelato function to begin churning.

7. Once the churning process is complete, your Chocolate-Hazelnut Gelato is ready to be savored. Serve it immediately, and relish the harmonious blend of chocolate and hazelnuts.

PREP TIP:

To toast hazelnuts, place them in a dry skillet over medium heat. Stir constantly until they become fragrant and lightly browned, then remove from heat and let them cool before chopping.

Sorbets

Mango Sorbet

SERVES 4

Escape to a tropical paradise with the refreshing delight of Mango Sorbet. This vibrant frozen treat captures the sweet and sunny essence of ripe mangoes in every spoonful.

PREP TIME: 15 minutes / Freeze time: 4 hours

FUNCTION: Sorbet

TOOLS NEEDED: Mixing bowl, whisk or rubber spatula

Ingredients

- 4 ripe mangoes, peeled, pitted, and diced
- 1/2 cup granulated sugar
- 1/4 cup freshly squeezed lime juice
- 1/4 cup water

Instructions

1. Begin by preparing the mangoes. Peel, pit, and dice the ripe mangoes, collecting them in a mixing bowl.

2. In a separate bowl, combine the granulated sugar, freshly squeezed lime juice, and water. Stir until the sugar is completely dissolved, creating a sweet and tangy syrup.

3. Pour the syrup over the diced mangoes in the mixing bowl.

4. Using a whisk or rubber spatula, gently fold the mango pieces into the syrup until they are well coated.

5. Transfer the mango and syrup mixture to a blender. Blend until you achieve a smooth and creamy consistency.

6. Once blended, pour the mango sorbet base into a CREAMi Pint and seal it with the storage lid. Freeze for a minimum of 4 hours or until the sorbet is firm.

7. After the freezing period, take the CREAMi Pint out and remove the lid. Put the CREAMi pint in the outer bowl. Ensure that the Creamerizer Paddle is attached to the lid of the outer bowl and lock the assembly into place.

8. Position the bowl onto the base and turn the handle towards the right in order to secure it. Select the Sorbet function to initiate the churning process.

9. Once the churning is complete, your Mango Sorbet is ready to be savored. Serve it immediately in chilled bowls or garnish with a slice of fresh mango for an extra touch of tropical goodness.

PREP TIP:

For a creamier texture, you can add a small amount of coconut milk to the mango sorbet base before blending.

Raspberry Sorbet

SERVES 4

Raspberry Sorbet is a refreshing and vibrant frozen dessert that captures the essence of ripe, juicy raspberries. This delightful sorbet is the perfect balance of sweet and tangy, making it a delightful treat for any occasion.

PREP TIME: 15 minutes / Freeze time: 4 hours

FUNCTION: Sorbet

TOOLS NEEDED: Mixing bowl, whisk or rubber spatula

Ingredients

- 3 cups fresh raspberries
- 1 cup granulated sugar
- 2 tablespoons freshly squeezed lemon juice
- 1/2 cup water

Instructions

1. Begin by preparing the raspberries. Rinse them thoroughly under cold water and then place them in a mixing bowl.

2. Using a fork or a potato masher, gently mash the raspberries to release their juices. You want to achieve a slightly chunky puree.

3. In a separate saucepan, combine the granulated sugar and water. Heat over medium heat, stirring constantly, until the sugar is fully dissolved. This will create a simple syrup.

4. Once the simple syrup is ready, remove it from the heat and allow it to cool to room temperature.

5. Add the freshly squeezed lemon juice to the raspberry puree and stir to combine.

6. Pour the simple syrup into the raspberry mixture and mix thoroughly. This sweetens and balances the tartness of the raspberries.

7. Transfer the raspberry sorbet mixture to a CREAMi Pint and seal it with the storage lid. Freeze for a minimum of 4 hours to achieve the ideal sorbet texture.

8. After the freezing period, take the CREAMi Pint out and remove the lid. Put the CREAMi pint in the outer bowl. Ensure that the Creamerizer Paddle is attached to the lid of the outer bowl and lock the assembly into place.

9. Position the bowl onto the base and turn the handle towards the right in order to secure it. Select the Sorbet function to initiate the churning process.

10.   Once the churning is complete, your Raspberry Sorbet is ready to be enjoyed. Serve it immediately in chilled bowls for a burst of raspberry goodness.

PREP TIP:

For a smoother sorbet, strain the raspberry puree through a fine-mesh sieve before adding the simple syrup and lemon juice.

Lemon Sorbet

SERVES 4

Delight in the zesty and refreshing flavors of Lemon Sorbet. This palate-cleansing frozen treat is the perfect balance of tart and sweet, making it a splendid choice for a light and citrusy dessert.

PREP TIME: 15 minutes / Freeze time: 4 hours

FUNCTION: Sorbet

TOOLS NEEDED: Mixing bowl, whisk or rubber spatula

Ingredients

- 2 cups freshly squeezed lemon juice (about 10-12 lemons)
- 1 cup granulated sugar
- 1 cup water
- 1 tablespoon lemon zest (from organic lemons)
- 1 teaspoon pure vanilla extract

Instructions

1. Begin by making a simple syrup. In a saucepan, combine the granulated sugar and water. Heat over medium-low heat, stirring continuously, until the sugar has completely dissolved and the mixture becomes clear. Remove from heat and let it cool to room temperature.

2. While the simple syrup is cooling, zest some organic lemons to get about 1 tablespoon of lemon zest. Ensure you only use the outer, fragrant part of the lemon zest, avoiding the bitter white pith.

3. Once the simple syrup has cooled, add the freshly squeezed lemon juice and lemon zest to it. Stir to combine.

4. Stir in the pure vanilla extract to enhance the flavor profile.

5. Transfer the lemon sorbet mixture to a CREAMi Pint, seal it with the storage lid, and freeze for a minimum of 4 hours. This freezing time allows the sorbet to set into a delightful texture.

6. After the freezing period, take the CREAMi Pint out and remove the lid. Put the CREAMi pint in the outer bowl. Ensure that the Creamerizer Paddle is attached to the lid of the outer bowl and lock the assembly into place.

7. Position the bowl onto the base and turn the handle towards the right in order to secure it. Select the Sorbet function to start the churning process.

8. Once the churning is complete, your Lemon Sorbet is ready to be enjoyed. Serve it in chilled bowls or glasses to relish the vibrant citrus burst.

PREP TIP:

For an extra pop of lemony flavor and an appealing presentation, garnish your Lemon Sorbet with a twist of fresh lemon peel.

Watermelon Sorbet

SERVES 4

Escape the heat with the ultimate summer delight, Watermelon Sorbet. This recipe captures the pure essence of watermelon in a cool and refreshing dessert that's perfect for hot days.

PREP TIME: 15 minutes / Freeze time: 4 hours

FUNCTION: Sorbet

TOOLS NEEDED: Blender, mixing bowl, rubber spatula

Ingredients

- 4 cups ripe watermelon, cubed and seeded
- 1/2 cup granulated sugar
- 2 tablespoons fresh lime juice
- Zest of 1 lime

Instructions

1. Start by preparing the watermelon. Cube the ripe watermelon and ensure it's seedless. You want the pure, sweet flesh for this sorbet.

2. In a blender, combine the cubed watermelon, granulated sugar, and fresh lime juice. Blend until you achieve a smooth and homogenous mixture.

3. Once blended, strain the mixture through a fine-mesh sieve into a mixing bowl. This step helps remove any remaining seeds or pulp, leaving you with a pure watermelon liquid.

4. Add the zest of one lime to the watermelon mixture. This zest will infuse the sorbet with a subtle, citrusy aroma.

5. Mix the zest into the watermelon mixture until it's well incorporated.

6. Transfer the watermelon mixture to a CREAMi Pint and seal it with the storage lid. Freeze for a minimum of 4 hours, allowing the sorbet to firm up.

7. After the freezing time, take the CREAMi Pint out and remove the lid. Put the CREAMi pint in the outer bowl. Ensure the Creamerizer Paddle is attached to the lid of the outer bowl and lock the assembly into place.

8. Position the bowl onto the base and turn the handle towards the right in order to secure it. Select the Sorbet function to initiate the churning process.

9. Once the churning is complete, your Watermelon Sorbet is ready to be enjoyed. Serve it in chilled bowls or as a refreshing scoop in watermelon rind bowls for a fun summer presentation.

PREP TIP:

For added zing, garnish your Watermelon Sorbet with a thin lime slice before serving.

Pineapple Sorbet

SERVES 4

Experience the bright and refreshing taste of Pineapple Sorbet. This tropical delight is a burst of sunshine in every spoonful, making it an ideal treat for hot days or as a palate cleanser between courses.

PREP TIME: 15 minutes / Freeze time: 4 hours

FUNCTION: Sorbet

TOOLS NEEDED: Mixing bowl, whisk or rubber spatula

Ingredients

- 4 cups fresh pineapple chunks (about 1 medium pineapple)
- 1 cup granulated sugar
- 1/4 cup freshly squeezed lime juice (from about 2-3 limes)
- 1/4 teaspoon salt
- Zest of 1 lime

Instructions

1. Begin by preparing the pineapple. Peel and core the pineapple, then cut it into chunks. You'll need about 4 cups of pineapple chunks.

2. In a mixing bowl, combine the fresh pineapple chunks and granulated sugar. Toss the pineapple and sugar together until the pineapple is evenly coated. Allow this mixture to sit for about 10-15 minutes. This resting period helps release the pineapple's natural juices.

3. After the resting period, transfer the pineapple and sugar mixture to a blender or food processor. Add the freshly squeezed lime juice, salt, and the zest of 1 lime.

4. Blend the ingredients until you have a smooth puree. This should take about 1-2 minutes.

5. Pour the pineapple puree into a CREAMi Pint, seal it with the storage lid, and place it in the freezer for a minimum of 4 hours. This freezing time is essential to achieve the ideal sorbet consistency.

6. Once the sorbet has sufficiently frozen, take the CREAMi Pint out and remove the lid. Put the CREAMi pint in the outer bowl. Ensure that the Creamerizer Paddle is attached to the lid of the outer bowl and lock the assembly into place.

7. Position the bowl onto the base and turn the handle towards the right in order to secure it. Select the Sorbet function to initiate the churning process.

8. Once the churning is complete, your Pineapple Sorbet is ready to be enjoyed. Serve it in a chilled bowl or even in hollowed-out pineapple halves for an extra tropical touch.

PREP TIP:

For an added burst of freshness, garnish your Pineapple Sorbet with a small wedge of fresh lime before serving.

Blackberry Sorbet

SERVES 4

Blackberry Sorbet is a delightful and refreshing frozen dessert that captures the natural sweetness and vibrant color of ripe blackberries. With its intense berry flavor and smooth texture, it's the perfect treat to cool down on a hot day or to enjoy as a palate cleanser between courses.

PREP TIME: 15 minutes / Freeze time: 4 hours

FUNCTION: Sorbet

TOOLS NEEDED: Mixing bowl, whisk or rubber spatula

Ingredients

- 2 cups fresh blackberries
- 3/4 cup of granulated sugar
- 1/4 cup water
- 1 tablespoon fresh lemon juice
- 1 teaspoon lemon zest

Instructions

1. Start by preparing the blackberries. Rinse them thoroughly under cold water and drain.

2. In a mixing bowl, combine the fresh blackberries and granulated sugar. Use a whisk or a rubber spatula to gently mash and stir the blackberries, allowing them to release their juices and mix with the sugar. Continue until the sugar is mostly dissolved, and the mixture becomes somewhat syrupy. This should take about 5 minutes.

3. Next, add the water, fresh lemon juice, and lemon zest to the blackberry mixture. Stir until everything is well combined.

4. Transfer this vibrant mixture to a blender or food processor. Blend until it's completely smooth and the blackberry seeds are no longer visible.

5. Strain the pureed blackberry mixture through a fine-mesh sieve into a clean bowl. This step helps remove any remaining seeds and ensures a silky-smooth sorbet.

6. Once strained, cover the bowl and refrigerate the mixture for at least 2 hours to chill it thoroughly.

7. After the chilling time, pour the blackberry mixture into a CREAMi Pint and seal it with the storage lid. Freeze for a minimum of 4 hours to allow the sorbet to firm up.

8. When you're ready to serve, take the CREAMi Pint out and remove the lid. Put the CREAMi pint in the outer bowl, ensuring that the Creamerizer Paddle is attached onto the lid of the outer bowl, and lock.

9. Position the bowl onto the base and turn the handle towards the right in order to secure it. Select the Sorbet function to initiate the churning process.

10. Once the churning is complete, your Blackberry Sorbet is ready to be enjoyed. Serve it in chilled bowls or dessert glasses for a refreshing and fruity treat.

PREP TIP:

For added visual appeal, garnish your Blackberry Sorbet with a few fresh blackberries and a twist of lemon zest before serving.

Grapefruit Sorbet

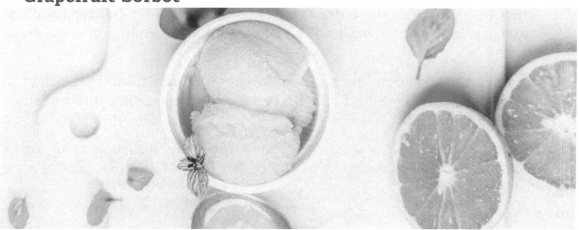

SERVES 4

Prepare to be refreshed by the tangy and zesty delight of Grapefruit Sorbet. This citrusy frozen treat captures the bright and vibrant essence of grapefruit, making it the perfect palate cleanser or a light and refreshing dessert.

PREP TIME: 15 minutes / Freeze time: 4 hours

FUNCTION: Sorbet

TOOLS NEEDED: Mixing bowl, whisk or rubber spatula

Ingredients

- 2 cups freshly squeezed grapefruit juice (from about 4-5 grapefruits)
- 1 cup granulated sugar
- 1/4 cup water
- Zest of 1 grapefruit
- 1 tablespoon freshly squeezed lemon juice

Instructions

1. In a mixing bowl, combine the granulated sugar and water. Whip the sugar until completely dissolved to create a simple syrup.

2. Add the freshly squeezed grapefruit juice, grapefruit zest, and freshly squeezed lemon juice to the simple syrup. Mix until everything is thoroughly combined.

3. Transfer the grapefruit sorbet mixture to a CREAMi Pint and seal it with the storage lid. Freeze for a minimum of 4 hours to ensure the sorbet reaches the perfect consistency.

4. After the freezing time, take the CREAMi Pint out and remove the lid. Put the CREAMi pint in the outer bowl. Make sure the Creamerizer Paddle is attached to the outer bowl lid, and lock the lid assembly onto the outer bowl.

5. Position the bowl onto the base and turn the handle towards the right in order to secure it. Select the Sorbet function to initiate the churning process.

6. Once the churning is complete, your Grapefruit Sorbet is ready to be enjoyed. Serve it immediately in chilled bowls or as a refreshing interlude between courses.

PREP TIP:

For the best flavor, use freshly squeezed grapefruit juice. You can also adjust the sugar to your taste, adding more or less as desired.

Lychee Sorbet

SERVES 4

Delight in the exotic and refreshing taste of Lychee Sorbet. This sorbet captures the essence of ripe lychee fruits, offering a sweet and tangy flavor that's perfect for cooling down on a warm day.

PREP TIME: 15 minutes / Freeze time: 4 hours

FUNCTION: Sorbet

TOOLS NEEDED: Mixing bowl, whisk or rubber spatula

Ingredients

- 2 cups fresh lychee fruit, peeled, pitted, and pureed

- 1/2 cup granulated sugar

- 1/2 cup water

- 1 tablespoon fresh lime juice

- Zest of 1 lime

Instructions

1. Begin by preparing the lychee puree. Peel and pit the fresh lychee fruits, then puree them in a blender or food processor until smooth. Set aside.

2. In a small saucepan, combine the granulated sugar and water. Heat over medium-low heat, stirring constantly until the sugar is completely dissolved. Remove from heat and let the sugar syrup cool to room temperature.

3. Once the sugar syrup has cooled, add it to the lychee puree. Stir to combine.

4. Incorporate the fresh lime juice and the zest of one lime into the mixture. These ingredients will enhance the lychee's natural flavors and provide a delightful citrusy note.

5. Transfer the sorbet mixture to a CREAMi Pint, seal it with the storage lid, and freeze for a minimum of 4 hours. This freezing period is crucial for achieving the ideal sorbet texture.

6. After the freezing time, take the CREAMi Pint out and remove the lid. Put the CREAMi pint in the outer bowl. Make sure the Creamerizer Paddle is attached to the outer bowl lid, and lock the lid assembly onto the outer bowl.

7. Position the bowl onto the base and turn the handle towards the right in order to secure it. Select the Sorbet function to commence the churning process.

8. Once the churning is complete, your Lychee Sorbet is ready to be savored. Serve it immediately in chilled bowls or glasses to relish the tropical delight of this frozen treat.

PREP TIP:

For a more intense lime flavor, you can add a bit more fresh lime juice or zest to suit your taste.

Passionfruit Sorbet

SERVES 4

Experience a burst of tropical flavor with this Passionfruit Sorbet. It's a refreshing and tangy frozen dessert that captures the essence of ripe passionfruit. With its vibrant color and zesty taste, this sorbet is a delightful treat for hot days or as a palate cleanser between courses.

PREP TIME: 15 minutes / Freeze time: 4 hours

FUNCTION: Sorbet

TOOLS NEEDED: Mixing bowl, whisk or rubber spatula

Ingredients

- 1 cup fresh passionfruit pulp (about 6-8 ripe passionfruits)
- 1/2 cup granulated sugar
- 1/4 cup water
- 1 teaspoon fresh lime juice

Instructions

1. Start by preparing the passionfruit pulp. Cut the passionfruits in half, scoop out the pulp, and strain it to remove any seeds. You should have about 1 cup of fresh passionfruit pulp.

2. In a mixing bowl, combine the granulated sugar and water. Stir until the sugar is completely dissolved, creating a simple syrup.

3. Add the fresh passionfruit pulp to the simple syrup and mix well to combine.

4. Stir in the fresh lime juice to enhance the tangy flavor.

5. Transfer the passionfruit mixture to a CREAMi Pint and seal it with the storage lid. Freeze for a minimum of 4 hours to achieve the ideal sorbet consistency.

6. After the freezing period, take the CREAMi Pint out and remove the lid. Put the CREAMi pint in the outer bowl. Ensure that the Creamerizer Paddle is attached to the lid of the outer bowl and lock the assembly into place.

7. Position the bowl onto the base and turn the handle towards the right in order to secure it. Select the Sorbet function to start the churning process.

8. Once the churning is complete, your Passionfruit Sorbet is ready to be enjoyed. Serve it in chilled bowls or as a refreshing palate cleanser between courses during a special meal.

PREP TIP:

For an extra burst of freshness, consider adding a few finely grated lime zest as a garnish.

Pomegranate Sorbet

SERVES 4

Embark on a refreshing journey with the vibrant and tangy Pomegranate Sorbet. This delightful frozen dessert captures the essence of ripe pomegranates, offering a burst of fruity flavor with each spoonful.

PREP TIME: 15 minutes / Freeze time: 4 hours

FUNCTION: Sorbet

TOOLS NEEDED: Mixing bowl, whisk or rubber spatula

Ingredients

- 2 cups pomegranate juice (freshly squeezed or store-bought)

- 1/2 cup granulated sugar

- 1/4 cup water

- 1 tablespoon fresh lemon juice

- Zest of one lemon

- Pomegranate seeds and lemon slices for garnish (optional)

Instructions

1. In a mixing bowl, combine the pomegranate juice and granulated sugar. Whip the sugar until completely dissolved.

2. In a separate small saucepan, heat the water over medium heat until it just begins to simmer. Remove it from the heat.

3. Slowly pour the hot water into the pomegranate mixture, stirring continuously to combine.

4. Add the fresh lemon juice and the zest of one lemon to the mixture. Stir until the ingredients are well incorporated.

5. Transfer the sorbet base to a CREAMi Pint and seal it with the storage lid. Freeze for a minimum of 4 hours to achieve the desired sorbet consistency.

6. After the freezing period, take the CREAMi Pint out and remove the lid. Put the CREAMi pint in the outer bowl. Ensure that the Creamerizer Paddle is attached to the lid of the outer bowl and lock the assembly into place.

7. Position the bowl onto the base and turn the handle towards the right in order to secure it. Select the Sorbet function to initiate the churning process.

8. Once the sorbet has reached the ideal texture, it's ready to be enjoyed. Serve it immediately in chilled bowls or glasses. If desired, garnish with fresh pomegranate seeds and lemon slices for an extra burst of flavor and visual appeal.

PREP TIP:

For the most vibrant flavor, use freshly squeezed pomegranate juice. You can easily extract the juice from pomegranates by cutting them in half and juicing them with a citrus juicer or blender.

Cantaloupe Sorbet

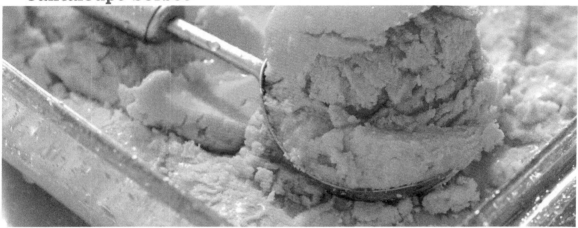

SERVES 4

Refreshingly sweet and bursting with the essence of ripe cantaloupe, this Cantaloupe Sorbet is the epitome of a summer dessert. It's a simple yet elegant treat that captures the pure flavor of the fruit.

PREP TIME: 15 minutes / Freeze time: 4 hours

FUNCTION: Sorbet

TOOLS NEEDED: Blender or food processor, mixing bowl, whisk or rubber spatula

Ingredients

- 1 ripe cantaloupe, peeled, seeded, and cubed
- 1/2 cup granulated sugar
- 1 tablespoon fresh lemon juice
- Zest of 1 lemon

Instructions

1. Begin by preparing the cantaloupe. Peel the cantaloupe, remove the seeds, and cut it into small, evenly sized cubes.

2. In a blender or food processor, add the cubed cantaloupe, granulated sugar, fresh lemon juice, and lemon zest. Blend until you have a smooth and uniform puree.

3. Transfer the cantaloupe puree to a mixing bowl, and use a whisk or rubber spatula to ensure that the sugar is fully dissolved in the puree. This step is important for achieving the right texture in your sorbet.

4. Once the mixture is well-combined, transfer it to a CREAMi Pint and secure the lid. Place it in the freezer for a minimum of 4 hours. This freezing time allows the sorbet to set and develop its delightful consistency.

5. After the freezing period, remove the CREAMi Pint out of the freezer, then take off the lid. Put the CREAMi pint in the outer bowl, ensuring that the Creamerizer Paddle is attached onto the lid of the outer bowl, and lock.

6. Position the bowl onto the base and turn the handle towards the right in order to secure it. Select the Sorbet function to begin churning.

7. Once the churning process is complete, your Cantaloupe Sorbet is ready to be enjoyed. Serve it immediately to savor the pure essence of ripe cantaloupe.

PREP TIP:

For a slightly different twist, try adding a splash of white rum to the puree for an adult-friendly version.

Apple Cider Sorbet

SERVES 4

Embrace the crisp and refreshing flavors of autumn with this Apple Cider Sorbet. It's like sipping on the essence of a freshly picked apple. Perfect for when you want a light and fruity frozen treat.

PREP TIME: 15 minutes / Freeze time: 4 hours

FUNCTION: Sorbet

TOOLS NEEDED: Mixing bowl, whisk or rubber spatula

Ingredients

- 2 cups fresh apple cider
- 1/2 cup granulated sugar
- 1/4 cup water
- 1 teaspoon lemon juice
- 1/2 teaspoon ground cinnamon
- 1/4 teaspoon ground nutmeg

Instructions

1. In a mixing bowl, combine the fresh apple cider, granulated sugar, water, lemon juice, ground cinnamon, and ground nutmeg. Whip the sugar until completely dissolved and the spices are evenly distributed.

2. Once the mixture is well combined, transfer it to a CREAMi Pint and secure the lid. Freeze for a minimum of 4 hours. This freezing time allows the sorbet to set and develop its delightful texture.

3. After the freezing period, retrieve the CREAMi Pint out of the freezer, then take off the lid. Put the CREAMi pint in the outer bowl, ensuring the Creamerizer Paddle is attached onto the lid of the outer bowl, and lock.

4. Position the bowl onto the base and turn the handle towards the right in order to secure it. Select the Sorbet function to begin churning.

5. Once the churning process is complete, your Apple Cider Sorbet is ready to be enjoyed. Serve it immediately, savoring the crisp apple flavors and subtle spice notes.

PREP TIP:

For a touch of warmth, consider adding a pinch of ground cloves to enhance the autumn spice profile.

Milkshakes

Classic Milkshake

SERVES 2

Indulge in the timeless delight of a Classic Milkshake. This frosty, creamy beverage is a true classic that never goes out of style. Plus, with the help of the Ninja CREAMi, you can achieve the perfect milkshake consistency in no time.

PREP TIME: 5 minutes / FUNCTION: Milkshake

TOOLS NEEDED: Ninja CREAMi

Ingredients

- 2 cups vanilla ice cream
- 1 cup of whole milk
- 1/4 cup granulated sugar (adjust to taste)
- 1 teaspoon pure vanilla extract

Instructions

1. Begin by assembling your clean and ready-to-use Ninja CREAMi.

2. In the pitcher of the Ninja CREAMi, combine the vanilla ice cream, whole milk, granulated sugar, and pure vanilla extract.

3. Secure the pitcher onto the base of the Ninja CREAMi.

4. Select the Milkshake function on the Ninja CREAMi. This function is designed specifically to create the perfect milkshake consistency, expertly blending all the ingredients into a creamy, frothy delight.

5. Allow the Ninja CREAMi to work its magic. It will automatically blend and churn the ingredients until you have a smooth and thick milkshake.

6. Once the Milkshake function is complete, carefully pour the creamy milkshake into two tall glasses.

7. For that classic milkshake aesthetic, you can optionally garnish each milkshake with a generous dollop of whipped cream and top it off with a maraschino cherry.

8. Serve immediately with a straw and savor the nostalgic pleasure of a Classic Milkshake.

PREP TIP:

Taste the milkshake before serving and adjust the sugar to your preference. You can also get creative by adding chocolate syrup, caramel, or other toppings for a customized twist.

Oreo Milkshake

SERVES 2

If you're a fan of the classic Oreo cookie, you're in for a treat. This Oreo Milkshake combines the beloved chocolatey crunch of Oreos with the creamy indulgence of a milkshake. Using the Ninja CREAMi, you'll achieve a perfect blend every time.

PREP TIME: 5 minutes / FUNCTION: Milkshake

TOOLS NEEDED: Ninja CREAMi

Ingredients

- 8 Oreo cookies

- 2 cups vanilla ice cream

- 1 cup of whole milk

- 1/4 cup granulated sugar (adjust to taste)

- 1 teaspoon pure vanilla extract

Instructions

1. Start by preparing your Ninja CREAMi. Ensure that it's clean and ready to use.

2. Take 4 of the Oreo cookies and break them into smaller pieces. These will be blended into the milkshake for that delightful Oreo crunch.

3. In the pitcher of the Ninja CREAMi, combine the broken Oreo cookies, vanilla ice cream, whole milk, granulated sugar, and pure vanilla extract.

4. Secure the pitcher onto the base of the Ninja CREAMi.

5. Select the Milkshake function on the Ninja CREAMi. This function is tailored to achieve the ideal milkshake consistency, blending all the ingredients into a creamy and decadent treat.

6. Allow the Ninja CREAMi to work its magic. It will automatically blend and churn the ingredients until you have a smooth and rich Oreo Milkshake.

7. Once the Milkshake function is complete, you'll have a thick and creamy milkshake with Oreo goodness.

8. Crush the remaining 4 Oreo cookies into smaller pieces. Sprinkle these crushed Oreos on top of the milkshake for an extra layer of Oreo delight.

9. Serve your Oreo Milkshake immediately with a straw and perhaps an extra Oreo cookie for garnish.

PREP TIP:

Feel free to adjust the sugar according to your taste preferences. If you want your milkshake even thicker, you can add more ice cream.

Peanut Butter Banana Milkshake

SERVES 2

Experience the delicious fusion of creamy peanut butter and ripe bananas in this Peanut Butter Banana Milkshake. With the Ninja CREAMi, you can create a lusciously smooth and satisfying milkshake that's perfect for a quick treat.

PREP TIME: 5 minutes / FUNCTION: Milkshake

TOOLS NEEDED: Ninja CREAMi

Ingredients

- 2 ripe bananas
- 1/4 cup creamy peanut butter
- 2 cups vanilla ice cream
- 1 cup of whole milk
- 2 tablespoons honey (adjust to taste)

Instructions

1. Start by assembling your Ninja CREAMi, ensuring it's clean and ready to use.

2. Peel the ripe bananas and break them into smaller chunks for easier blending.

3. In the pitcher of the Ninja CREAMi, combine the banana chunks, creamy peanut butter, vanilla ice cream, whole milk, and honey.

4. Secure the pitcher onto the base of the Ninja CREAMi.

5. Select the Milkshake function on the Ninja CREAMi. This function is designed specifically to create the perfect milkshake consistency, blending all the ingredients into a creamy and indulgent treat.

6. Allow the Ninja CREAMi to work its magic. It will automatically blend and churn the ingredients until you have a smooth and thick Peanut Butter Banana Milkshake.

7. Taste the milkshake and adjust the sweetness by adding more honey if desired. Blend briefly to incorporate any additional sweetness.

8. Carefully pour the creamy milkshake into two tall glasses.

9. For an extra touch of indulgence, you can optionally drizzle a little extra peanut butter on top and garnish with banana slices or a sprinkle of crushed peanuts.

10. Serve immediately with a straw and savor the delightful combination of peanut butter and banana flavors in this satisfying milkshake.

PREP TIP:

For a thicker milkshake, consider using frozen banana chunks.

Nutella Milkshake

SERVES 2

Indulge in the heavenly blend of rich chocolate-hazelnut goodness with this Nutella Milkshake. Creamy and decadent, it's a delightful treat that's incredibly easy to whip up with the Ninja CREAMi.

PREP TIME: 5 minutes / FUNCTION: Milkshake

TOOLS NEEDED: Ninja CREAMi

Ingredients

- 2 cups vanilla ice cream
- 1/2 cup whole milk
- 1/4 cup Nutella (chocolate-hazelnut spread)
- 2 tablespoons granulated sugar (adjust to taste)
- Whipped cream (for garnish, optional)
- Chopped hazelnuts (for garnish, optional)

Instructions

1. Ensure your Ninja CREAMi is clean and ready for use.
2. In the pitcher of the Ninja CREAMi, combine the vanilla ice cream, whole milk, Nutella, and granulated sugar.
3. Secure the pitcher onto the base of the Ninja CREAMi.
4. Select the Milkshake function on the Ninja CREAMi. This function is designed specifically to create a lusciously creamy milkshake by blending all the ingredients to perfection.
5. Allow the Ninja CREAMi to work its magic. It will automatically blend and churn the ingredients until you have a smooth and indulgent Nutella Milkshake.
6. Once the Milkshake function is complete, pour the creamy Nutella Milkshake into two tall glasses.
7. For an extra touch of indulgence, you can garnish each milkshake with a dollop of whipped cream and a sprinkle of chopped hazelnuts.
8. Serve immediately with a straw and savor the irresistible combination of chocolate and hazelnut in this Nutella Milkshake.

PREP TIP:

Taste the milkshake before serving and adjust the sugar to your preference. You can also drizzle some Nutella on top for an extra Nutella kick!

Vegan Chocolate Milkshake

SERVES 2

Indulge in the rich, chocolaty goodness of a Vegan Chocolate Milkshake. This dairy-free delight is not only delicious but also perfect for those following a vegan lifestyle. With the Ninja CREAMi, you can create a creamy vegan milkshake that's just as satisfying as the traditional version.

PREP TIME: 5 minutes / FUNCTION: Milkshake

TOOLS NEEDED: Ninja CREAMi

Ingredients

- 2 cups vegan chocolate ice cream
- 1 cup unsweetened almond milk (or any plant-based milk of your choice)
- 1/4 cup pure maple syrup (adjust to taste)
- 2 tablespoons unsweetened cocoa powder
- 1 teaspoon pure vanilla extract

Instructions

1. Start by assembling your clean and ready-to-use Ninja CREAMi.

2. In the pitcher of the Ninja CREAMi, combine the vegan chocolate ice cream, unsweetened almond milk, pure maple syrup, unsweetened cocoa powder, and pure vanilla extract.

3. Secure the pitcher onto the base of the Ninja CREAMi.

4. Select the Milkshake function on the Ninja CREAMi. This function is designed specifically to create a smooth and creamy milkshake consistency, ensuring all the ingredients are perfectly blended.

5. Allow the Ninja CREAMi to work its magic. It will automatically blend and churn the ingredients until you have a luscious vegan chocolate milkshake.

6. Once the Milkshake function is complete, carefully pour the creamy vegan chocolate milkshake into two tall glasses.

7. If you like, you can top each milkshake with a dollop of vegan whipped cream and a dusting of cocoa powder for added decadence.

8. Serve immediately with a straw and enjoy the guilt-free pleasure of a Vegan Chocolate Milkshake.

PREP TIP:

Taste the milkshake before serving and adjust the sweetness with more maple syrup if needed. You can also add dairy-free chocolate chips or cocoa nibs for extra texture and flavor.

Strawberry Cheesecake Milkshake

SERVES 2

Experience the perfect blend of creamy cheesecake and luscious strawberries in this Strawberry Cheesecake Milkshake. With the Ninja CREAMi, you can effortlessly transform these classic flavors into a delightful frozen treat.

PREP TIME: 10 minutes / FUNCTION: Milkshake

TOOLS NEEDED: Ninja CREAMi

Ingredients

- 2 cups vanilla ice cream

- 1 cup of whole milk

- 1/2 cup fresh or frozen strawberries, hulled and halved

- 1/4 cup cream cheese, softened

- 1/4 cup granulated sugar (adjust to taste)

- 1 teaspoon pure vanilla extract

- Graham cracker crumbs (for garnish)

Instructions

1. Start by assembling your clean and ready-to-use Ninja CREAMi.

2. In the pitcher of the Ninja CREAMi, combine the vanilla ice cream, whole milk, fresh or frozen strawberries, softened cream cheese, granulated sugar, and pure vanilla extract.

3. Secure the pitcher onto the base of the Ninja CREAMi.

4. Select the Milkshake function on the Ninja CREAMi. This function is designed to expertly blend and churn the ingredients into a creamy, dreamy milkshake.

5. Allow the Ninja CREAMi to work its magic. It will automatically mix the ingredients until you have a smooth and luscious milkshake.

6. Once the Milkshake function is complete, it's time to serve.

7. To enhance the strawberry cheesecake experience, optionally rim each serving glass with graham cracker crumbs. You can do this by dipping the rim of each glass into a shallow dish of crushed graham crackers.

8. Carefully pour the Strawberry Cheesecake Milkshake into the prepared glasses.

9. For an extra touch of indulgence, you can garnish the milkshakes with a dollop of whipped cream and a fresh strawberry on top.

10. Serve immediately with a straw and savor the delightful combination of cheesecake and strawberries in this heavenly milkshake.

PREP TIP:

Feel free to adjust the sugar to your taste preference. If you prefer a thicker milkshake, add more ice cream; for a thinner consistency, add more milk.

Caramel Apple Milkshake

SERVES 2

Experience the sweet and tangy delight of a Caramel Apple Milkshake. This refreshing blend of flavors captures the essence of a caramel-drenched apple, making it the perfect treat for any occasion.

PREP TIME: 10 minutes / FUNCTION: Milkshake

TOOLS NEEDED: Ninja CREAMi

Ingredients

- 2 medium apples, peeled, cored, and diced
- 2 cups vanilla ice cream
- 1 cup of whole milk
- 1/4 cup caramel sauce (plus extra for drizzling)
- 2 tablespoons granulated sugar (adjust to taste)
- 1/2 teaspoon ground cinnamon
- Whipped cream (for garnish, optional)
- Sliced apples (for garnish, optional)

Instructions

1. Begin by assembling your clean and ready-to-use Ninja CREAMi.

2. In the pitcher of the Ninja CREAMi, combine the diced apples, vanilla ice cream, whole milk, caramel sauce, granulated sugar, and ground cinnamon.

3. Secure the pitcher onto the base of the Ninja CREAMi.

4. Select the Milkshake function on the Ninja CREAMi. This function is designed specifically to create the perfect milkshake consistency, blending all the ingredients into a creamy, luscious treat.

5. Allow the Ninja CREAMi to work its magic. It will automatically blend and churn the ingredients until you have a smooth and indulgent Caramel Apple Milkshake.

6. Once the Milkshake function is complete, carefully pour the delightful milkshake into two tall glasses.

7. Drizzle additional caramel sauce on top of each milkshake for an extra layer of caramel goodness.

8. If you desire, garnish each milkshake with a swirl of whipped cream and a thin apple slice for a beautiful presentation.

9. Serve immediately with a straw and enjoy the delightful fusion of caramel and apple flavors in every sip.

PREP TIP:

Adjust the sugar to your taste preference, as the sweetness of the milkshake will depend on the ripeness of the apples and the caramel sauce you use.

S'mores Milkshake

SERVES 2

Experience the nostalgic joy of a campfire treat in the form of a S'mores Milkshake. This delightful concoction combines the flavors of toasted marshmallows, rich chocolate, and graham crackers, all blended into a creamy milkshake. Thanks to the Ninja CREAMi, you can enjoy this indulgence without the need for a campfire.

PREP TIME: 10 minutes / FUNCTION: Milkshake

TOOLS NEEDED: Ninja CREAMi

Ingredients

- 2 cups vanilla ice cream
- 1 cup of whole milk
- 2 tablespoons chocolate syrup
- 2 tablespoons crushed graham crackers
- 2 tablespoons mini marshmallows, plus extra for garnish
- 1 teaspoon pure vanilla extract
- Whipped cream (optional)
- Chocolate shavings (optional)
- Additional crushed graham crackers (optional)

Instructions

1. Begin by assembling your Ninja CREAMi, ensuring it's clean and ready to use.

2. In the pitcher of the Ninja CREAMi, combine the vanilla ice cream, whole milk, chocolate syrup, crushed graham crackers, mini marshmallows, and pure vanilla extract.

3. Secure the pitcher onto the base of the Ninja CREAMi.

4. Select the Milkshake function on the Ninja CREAMi. This function is tailored to create a perfectly blended milkshake, ensuring that all the ingredients come together into a creamy, flavorful mixture.

5. Allow the Ninja CREAMi to work its magic. It will automatically blend and churn the ingredients until you have a smooth and dreamy S'mores Milkshake.

6. Once the Milkshake function is complete, you're ready to serve. Carefully pour the S'mores Milkshake into two tall glasses.

7. For an extra touch of decadence, consider topping each milkshake with a generous swirl of whipped cream, a sprinkle of chocolate shavings, additional crushed graham crackers, and a few mini marshmallows.

8. Don't forget the straw! Serve your S'mores Milkshake with a straw and enjoy the delightful blend of campfire flavors in a refreshing milkshake.

PREP TIP:

You can get creative by drizzling extra chocolate syrup on the inside of each glass before pouring in the milkshake for an even more indulgent experience.

Mint Oreo Milkshake

SERVES 2

Experience the refreshing zing of mint and the delightful crunch of Oreo cookies in this Mint Oreo Milkshake. Thanks to the Ninja CREAMi, you can whip up this cool and indulgent treat in no time.

PREP TIME: 5 minutes / FUNCTION: Milkshake

TOOLS NEEDED: Ninja CREAMi

Ingredients

- 2 cups mint chocolate chip ice cream
- 1 cup of whole milk
- 4 Oreo cookies, crushed
- 1/4 cup granulated sugar (adjust to taste)
- 1/2 teaspoon peppermint extract (adjust to taste)

Instructions

1. Start by ensuring your Ninja CREAMi is clean and ready for use.

2. In the pitcher of the Ninja CREAMi, combine the mint chocolate chip ice cream, whole milk, crushed Oreo cookies, granulated sugar, and peppermint extract.

3. Secure the pitcher onto the base of the Ninja CREAMi.

4. Select the Milkshake function on the Ninja CREAMi. This function is tailored to create the perfect milkshake consistency, seamlessly blending all the ingredients into a creamy and delightful treat.

5. Allow the Ninja CREAMi to work its magic. It will automatically blend and churn the ingredients until you have a smooth and thick Mint Oreo Milkshake.

6. Once the Milkshake function is complete, carefully pour the minty, cookie-infused milkshake into two tall glasses.

7. For an extra touch of indulgence, you can optionally top each milkshake with whipped cream and garnish it with additional crushed Oreo cookies.

8. Serve immediately with a straw and enjoy the invigorating and crunchy pleasure of a Mint Oreo Milkshake.

PREP TIP:

Taste the milkshake before serving and adjust the sugar and peppermint extract to your preference for sweetness and mintiness.

Coffee Toffee Milkshake

SERVES 2

Elevate your milkshake experience with the irresistible blend of coffee and toffee. This Coffee Toffee Milkshake combines the robust flavors of coffee with the sweet crunch of toffee for a delightful treat that's perfect for coffee lovers.

PREP TIME: 5 minutes / FUNCTION: Milkshake

TOOLS NEEDED: Ninja CREAMi

Ingredients

- 2 cups coffee ice cream
- 1 cup of whole milk
- 1/4 cup toffee bits
- 1 tablespoon instant coffee granules
- 2 tablespoons granulated sugar (adjust to taste)
- Whipped cream and additional toffee bits for garnish (optional)

Instructions

1. Ensure your Ninja CREAMi is clean and ready for use.

2. In the pitcher of the Ninja CREAMi, combine the coffee ice cream, whole milk, toffee bits, instant coffee granules, and granulated sugar.

3. Secure the pitcher onto the base of the Ninja CREAMi.

4. Select the Milkshake function on the Ninja CREAMi. This function is designed to create a perfect milkshake consistency, expertly blending all the ingredients into a creamy and frothy delight.

5. Allow the Ninja CREAMi to work its magic. It will automatically blend and churn the ingredients until you have a smooth and thick Coffee Toffee Milkshake.

6. Once the Milkshake function is complete, carefully pour the indulgent milkshake into two tall glasses.

7. For an added touch of indulgence, you can optionally garnish each milkshake with a generous swirl of whipped cream and a sprinkle of toffee bits.

8. Serve your Coffee Toffee Milkshake immediately with a straw, and enjoy the harmonious blend of coffee and toffee flavors.

PREP TIP:

Taste the milkshake before serving and adjust the sugar to your preference. You can also drizzle caramel sauce over the whipped cream for an extra layer of sweetness.

Smoothie Bowls

Acai Smoothie Bowl

SERVES 2

Experience a burst of tropical flavors with this refreshing Acai Bowl. Crafted to perfection with the Ninja CREAMi ice cream maker, it's a delightful combination of creamy acai, fresh fruits, and wholesome toppings.

PREP TIME: 10 minutes / Freeze time: 2 hours

FUNCTION: Smoothie Bowl

TOOLS NEEDED: Ninja CREAMi ice cream maker, blender

Ingredients

- 2 packs frozen unsweetened acai puree (about 200g each)
- 1 ripe banana
- 1/2 cup frozen mixed berries
- 1/4 cup almond milk (or your choice of milk)
- 2 tablespoons honey or maple syrup (optional, for sweetness)
- Toppings: Sliced bananas, fresh berries, granola, chia seeds, shredded coconut, and honey

Instructions

1. Start by allowing the frozen acai puree packs to thaw slightly for about 5 minutes. This will make it easier to blend.

2. In a blender, combine the thawed acai puree, ripe banana, frozen mixed berries, almond milk, and sweetener (if desired). Blend until you achieve a smooth, thick, and creamy consistency.

3. Pour the acai mixture into a clean CREAMi Pint, seal it with the storage lid, and place it in the freezer for approximately 2 hours. This short freezing time will help the acai mixture thicken into a creamy texture suitable for a smoothie bowl.

4. After the freezing time, take the CREAMi Pint out and remove the lid. Put the CREAMi pint in the outer bowl, ensuring the Creamerizer Paddle is attached onto the lid of the outer bowl, and lock.

5. Position the bowl components on the motor-base and secure by turning the handle to the right. Select the Smoothie Bowl function to create a smooth and creamy acai base.

6. Once the machine has completed the process, serve your Acai Bowl immediately. Top it with sliced bananas, fresh berries, granola, chia seeds, shredded coconut, and a drizzle of honey to your heart's content.

PREP TIP:

For an extra chilled bowl, place your serving bowls in the freezer for a few minutes before serving.

Tropical Smoothie Bowl

SERVES 2

Transport yourself to a tropical paradise with this delightful Tropical Smoothie Bowl. Crafted to perfection with the Ninja CREAMi ice cream maker, it's a symphony of exotic fruits and wholesome toppings.

PREP TIME: 10 minutes / Freeze time: 2 hours

FUNCTION: Smoothie Bowl

TOOLS NEEDED: Ninja CREAMi ice cream maker, blender

Ingredients

- 1 cup frozen mango chunks

- 1 cup frozen pineapple chunks

- 1 ripe banana

- 1/2 cup coconut milk

- 2 tablespoons honey or maple syrup (optional, for sweetness)

- Toppings: Sliced kiwi, fresh berries, diced pineapple, shredded coconut, chia seeds, and a sprinkle of granola

Instructions

1. Begin by placing the frozen mango chunks, frozen pineapple chunks, ripe banana, coconut milk, and sweetener (if desired) into a blender.

2. Blend the ingredients until you achieve a smooth and creamy tropical smoothie mixture. It should have a thick consistency suitable for a smoothie bowl.

3. Transfer the tropical smoothie mixture into a clean CREAMi Pint, seal it with the storage lid, and place it in the freezer for approximately 2 hours. This short freezing time will help thicken the smoothie into a creamy texture perfect for a smoothie bowl.

4. After the freezing time, take the CREAMi Pint out and remove the lid. Put the CREAMi pint in the outer bowl, ensuring the Creamerizer Paddle is attached onto the lid of the outer bowl, and lock.

5. Position the bowl components on the motor-base and secure by turning the handle to the right. Select the Smoothie Bowl function to create a silky and luscious tropical smoothie base.

6. Once the machine has completed the process, serve your Tropical Smoothie Bowl immediately. Top it with sliced kiwi, fresh berries, diced pineapple, shredded coconut, chia seeds, and a sprinkle of granola for an extra burst of tropical goodness.

PREP TIP:

For a creamier texture, you can add a tablespoon of Greek yogurt to the smoothie mixture before blending.

Green Smoothie Bowl

SERVES 2

Delight in the goodness of greens with this invigorating Green Smoothie Bowl. Crafted with the Ninja CREAMi ice cream maker, it's a refreshing blend of leafy vegetables and wholesome toppings.

PREP TIME: 10 minutes / Freeze time: 2 hours

FUNCTION: Smoothie Bowl

TOOLS NEEDED: Ninja CREAMi ice cream maker, blender

Ingredients

- 2 cups fresh spinach leaves
- 1 ripe banana
- 1/2 ripe avocado
- 1/2 cup frozen pineapple chunks
- 1/2 cup coconut water (or your choice of liquid)
- 1 tablespoon honey or maple syrup (optional, for sweetness)
- Toppings: Sliced banana, kiwi slices, fresh berries, granola, chia seeds, and shredded coconut

Instructions

1. Begin by preparing the green smoothie base. In a blender, combine the fresh spinach leaves, ripe banana, ripe avocado, frozen pineapple chunks, and coconut water (or your choice of liquid).

2. Blend until you achieve a smooth and vibrant green mixture. If you prefer a sweeter taste, you can add honey or maple syrup to taste and blend again.

3. Transfer the green smoothie mixture into a clean CREAMi Pint, seal it with the storage lid, and place it in the freezer for approximately 2 hours. This brief freezing period will help the mixture thicken into a creamy consistency suitable for a smoothie bowl.

4. After the freezing time, take the CREAMi Pint out and remove the lid. Put the CREAMi pint in the outer bowl, ensuring the Creamerizer Paddle is attached onto the lid of the outer bowl, and lock.

5. Position the bowl onto the base and turn the handle towards the right in order to secure it. Select the Smoothie Bowl function to create a creamy and refreshing green smoothie base.

6. Once the machine has completed the process, serve your Green Smoothie Bowl immediately. Top it with sliced banana, kiwi slices, fresh berries, granola, chia seeds, and shredded coconut for added texture and flavor.

PREP TIP:

For a creamier consistency, you can add a frozen banana or extra avocado to the blender.

Berry Protein Smoothie Bowl

SERVES 2

Energize your day with the Berry Protein Smoothie Bowl, a perfect blend of vibrant berries and protein-packed goodness. Crafted with the Ninja CREAMi ice cream maker, this bowl offers a delightful combination of flavors and nutrients.

PREP TIME: 10 minutes / Freeze time: 2 hours

FUNCTION: Smoothie Bowl

TOOLS NEEDED: Ninja CREAMi ice cream maker, blender

Ingredients

- 1 cup frozen mixed berries (strawberries, blueberries, raspberries)
- 1 ripe banana
- 1/2 cup Greek yogurt
- 1/2 cup almond milk (or your choice of milk)
- 1 scoop vanilla protein powder
- 2 tablespoons honey or maple syrup (optional, for sweetness)
- Toppings: Fresh berries, sliced banana, granola, chia seeds, and honey

Instructions

1. Begin by placing the frozen mixed berries, ripe banana, Greek yogurt, almond milk, vanilla protein powder, and sweetener (if desired) in a blender.

2. Blend the ingredients until you achieve a smooth and creamy consistency. The protein powder not only adds a protein boost but also contributes to the thickness of the smoothie bowl.

3. Pour the smoothie mixture into a clean CREAMi Pint, seal it with the storage lid, and place it in the freezer for approximately 2 hours. This short freezing time will help the smoothie base thicken to the perfect texture for a smoothie bowl.

4. After the freezing time, take the CREAMi Pint out and remove the lid. Put the CREAMi pint in the outer bowl, ensuring the Creamerizer Paddle is attached onto the lid of the outer bowl, and lock.

5. Position the bowl components on the motor-base and secure by turning the handle to the right. Select the Smoothie Bowl function to create a smooth and creamy base.

6. Once the machine has completed the process, serve your Berry Protein Smoothie Bowl immediately. Top it with fresh berries, sliced banana, granola, chia seeds, and a drizzle of honey for added flavor and nutrition.

PREP TIP:

You can customize your smoothie bowl by adding your favorite nuts or seeds for extra crunch and nutrition.

Chocolate Avocado Smoothie Bowl

SERVES 2

Indulge in the creamy goodness of a Chocolate Avocado Smoothie Bowl. Crafted with the Ninja CREAMi ice cream maker, this bowl combines the richness of chocolate with the health benefits of avocado for a delightful treat.

PREP TIME: 10 minutes / Freeze time: 2 hours

FUNCTION: Smoothie Bowl

TOOLS NEEDED: Ninja CREAMi ice cream maker, blender

Ingredients

- 2 ripe avocados, peeled and pitted
- 2 tablespoons unsweetened cocoa powder
- 2 tablespoons honey or maple syrup (adjust to taste)
- 1 teaspoon pure vanilla extract
- 1/2 cup almond milk (or your choice of milk)

- Toppings: Sliced bananas, strawberries, chocolate chips, shredded coconut, and a drizzle of honey

Instructions

1. In a blender, combine the ripe avocados, unsweetened cocoa powder, honey (or maple syrup), pure vanilla extract, and almond milk. Blend until the mixture is smooth and creamy.

2. Pour the chocolate avocado mixture into a clean CREAMi Pint, seal it with the storage lid, and place it in the freezer for approximately 2 hours. This short freezing time will help the mixture thicken into a creamy texture suitable for a smoothie bowl.

3. After the freezing time, take the CREAMi Pint out and remove the lid. Put the CREAMi pint in the outer bowl, ensuring the Creamerizer Paddle is attached onto the lid of the outer bowl, and lock.

4. Position the bowl components on the motor-base and secure by turning the handle to the right. Select the Smoothie Bowl function to create a smooth and creamy chocolate avocado base.

5. Once the machine has completed the process, serve your Chocolate Avocado Smoothie Bowl immediately. Top it with sliced bananas, strawberries, chocolate chips, shredded coconut, and a drizzle of honey to add a delightful finishing touch.

PREP TIP:

For an extra creamy texture, ensure that the avocados are fully ripe.

Mango Tango Smoothie Bowl

SERVES 2

Indulge in the vibrant flavors of tropical mango with this refreshing Mango Tango Smoothie Bowl. Created with the Ninja CREAMi ice cream maker, it's a delightful blend of creamy mango goodness topped with an array of colorful, nutritious toppings.

PREP TIME: 10 minutes / Freeze time: 2 hours

FUNCTION: Smoothie Bowl

TOOLS NEEDED: Ninja CREAMi ice cream maker, blender

Ingredients

- 2 ripe mangoes, peeled, pitted, and diced
- 1/2 cup plain Greek yogurt
- 1/4 cup almond milk (or your choice of milk)
- 2 tablespoons honey or maple syrup (optional, for sweetness)
- Toppings: Sliced fresh mango, banana slices, kiwi slices, granola, sliced almonds, and a drizzle of honey

Instructions

1. Begin by preparing the mango. Peel, pit, and dice two ripe mangoes.

2. In a blender, combine the diced mangoes, plain Greek yogurt, almond milk, and sweetener (if desired). Blend until you achieve a smooth and creamy consistency.

3. Pour the mango mixture into a clean CREAMi Pint, seal it with the storage lid, and place it in the freezer for approximately 2 hours. This short freezing time will allow the mango mixture to thicken into a smoothie bowl consistency.

4. After the freezing time, take the CREAMi Pint out and remove the lid. Put the CREAMi pint in the outer bowl, ensuring the Creamerizer Paddle is attached onto the lid of the outer bowl, and lock.

5. Position the bowl components on the motor-base and secure by turning the handle to the right. Select the Smoothie Bowl function to create a creamy mango base.

6. Once the machine has completed the process, serve your Mango Tango Smoothie Bowl immediately. Top it with sliced fresh mango, banana slices, kiwi slices, granola, sliced almonds, and a drizzle of honey to your liking.

PREP TIP:

For an extra chilled bowl, place your serving bowls in the freezer for a few minutes before serving.

Peanut Butter and Jelly Smoothie Bowl

SERVES 2

Indulge in the nostalgic flavors of a classic childhood favorite, reimagined as a satisfying and wholesome Peanut Butter and Jelly Smoothie Bowl. Created with the Ninja CREAMi ice cream maker, this bowl combines the richness of peanut butter with the sweetness of jelly, all in a creamy smoothie form.

PREP TIME: 10 minutes / Freeze time: 2 hours

FUNCTION: Smoothie Bowl

TOOLS NEEDED: Ninja CREAMi ice cream maker, blender

Ingredients

- 2 ripe bananas
- 1/4 cup peanut butter
- 1/4 cup Greek yogurt
- 1/4 cup milk (of your choice)
- 2 tablespoons honey or maple syrup
- 1/2 cup frozen mixed berries
- Toppings: Sliced strawberries, grape jelly drizzle, chopped peanuts, and a sprinkle of oats

Instructions

1. Begin by peeling and slicing the ripe bananas. Place them in a blender.

2. Add the peanut butter, Greek yogurt, milk, and honey (or maple syrup) to the blender with the bananas.

3. Include the frozen mixed berries to the blender as well. Blend all the ingredients until you achieve a smooth and creamy consistency.

4. Transfer the smoothie mixture into a clean CREAMi Pint, seal it with the storage lid, and place it in the freezer for approximately 2 hours. This will help the smoothie thicken into a spoonable consistency ideal for a smoothie bowl.

5. After the freezing time, take the CREAMi Pint out and remove the lid. Put the CREAMi pint in the outer bowl, ensuring the Creamerizer Paddle is attached onto the lid of the outer bowl, and lock.

6. Position the bowl components on the motor-base and secure by turning the handle to the right. Select the Smoothie Bowl function to transform your smoothie into a creamy bowl.

7. Once the machine has completed the process, serve your Peanut Butter and Jelly Smoothie Bowl immediately. Top it with sliced strawberries, a delightful grape jelly drizzle, chopped peanuts for that perfect crunch, and a sprinkle of oats for added texture.

PREP TIP:

Feel free to customize your toppings with additional fruits, nuts, or seeds to suit your preference.

Blueberry Muffin Smoothie Bowl

SERVES 2

Indulge in the delightful flavors of a blueberry muffin, but in a healthier and cooler form with this Blueberry Muffin Smoothie Bowl. Prepared with the Ninja CREAMi ice cream maker, it's the perfect balance of fruity sweetness and satisfying textures.

PREP TIME: 10 minutes / Freeze time: 2 hours

FUNCTION: Smoothie Bowl

TOOLS NEEDED: Ninja CREAMi ice cream maker, blender

Ingredients

- 2 cups frozen blueberries
- 1 ripe banana
- 1/2 cup Greek yogurt
- 1/4 cup almond milk (or your choice of milk)
- 2 tablespoons honey or maple syrup (optional, for sweetness)
- 1/4 cup granola
- Fresh blueberries and sliced bananas for garnish

Instructions

1. In a blender, combine the frozen blueberries, ripe banana, Greek yogurt, almond milk, and sweetener (if desired). Blend until you achieve a smooth and creamy consistency.

2. Pour the blueberry mixture into a clean CREAMi Pint, seal it with the storage lid, and place it in the freezer for approximately 2 hours. This short freezing time will help thicken the mixture for a satisfying smoothie bowl.

3. After the freezing time, take the CREAMi Pint out and remove the lid. Put the CREAMi pint in the outer bowl, ensuring the Creamerizer Paddle is attached onto the lid of the outer bowl, and lock.

4. Position the bowl components on the motor-base and secure by turning the handle to the right. Select the Smoothie Bowl function to create a smooth and creamy blueberry muffin-inspired base.

5. Once the machine has completed the process, serve your Blueberry Muffin Smoothie Bowl immediately. Top it with granola, fresh blueberries, sliced bananas, and an extra drizzle of honey if desired.

PREP TIP:

For added crunch and flavor, you can toast the granola in the oven for a few minutes before using it as a topping.

Pumpkin Spice Smoothie Bowl

SERVES 2

Embrace the cozy flavors of fall with this Pumpkin Spice Smoothie Bowl. Crafted to perfection with the Ninja CREAMi ice cream maker, it's a warm and comforting blend of pumpkin, spices, and delightful toppings.

PREP TIME: 10 minutes / Freeze time: 2 hours

FUNCTION: Smoothie Bowl

TOOLS NEEDED: Ninja CREAMi ice cream maker, blender

Ingredients

- 1 cup canned pumpkin puree
- 1 ripe banana
- 1/2 cup Greek yogurt
- 1/4 cup almond milk (or your choice of milk)
- 2 tablespoons honey or maple syrup (optional, for sweetness)
- 1/2 teaspoon ground cinnamon
- 1/4 teaspoon ground nutmeg
- 1/4 teaspoon ground ginger
- 1/4 teaspoon ground cloves

- Toppings: Chopped pecans, pumpkin seeds, dried cranberries, a drizzle of honey, and a sprinkle of cinnamon

Instructions

1. In a blender, combine the canned pumpkin puree, ripe banana, Greek yogurt, almond milk, sweetener (if desired), and all the ground spices (cinnamon, nutmeg, ginger, and cloves). Blend until you achieve a smooth and creamy consistency.

2. Pour the pumpkin spice mixture into a clean CREAMi Pint, seal it with the storage lid, and place it in the freezer for approximately 2 hours. This brief freezing period will help thicken the smoothie into a perfect smoothie bowl texture.

3. After the freezing time, take the CREAMi Pint out and remove the lid. Put the CREAMi pint in the outer bowl, ensuring the Creamerizer Paddle is attached onto the lid of the outer bowl, and lock.

4. Position the bowl components on the motor-base and secure by turning the handle to the right. Select the Smoothie Bowl function to create a thick and indulgent pumpkin spice base.

5. Once the machine has completed the process, serve your Pumpkin Spice Smoothie Bowl immediately. Top it with chopped pecans, pumpkin seeds, dried cranberries, a drizzle of honey, and a sprinkle of cinnamon for added flavor and texture.

PREP TIP:

For a creamier texture, use frozen banana slices instead of a ripe banana.

Cherry Almond Smoothie Bowl

SERVES 2

Indulge in the vibrant flavors of sweet cherries and wholesome almonds with this Cherry Almond Smoothie Bowl. Crafted with the Ninja CREAMi ice cream maker, it's a delightful balance of fruity and nutty goodness.

PREP TIME: 10 minutes / Freeze time: 2 hours

FUNCTION: Smoothie Bowl

TOOLS NEEDED: Ninja CREAMi ice cream maker, blender

Ingredients

- 2 cups frozen sweet cherries
- 1 ripe banana
- 1/4 cup almond butter
- 1/2 cup almond milk (or your choice of milk)
- 2 tablespoons honey or maple syrup (optional, for sweetness)
- Toppings: Sliced almonds, fresh cherries, granola, chia seeds, and a drizzle of honey

Instructions

1. Begin by allowing the frozen sweet cherries to thaw slightly for about 5 minutes. This will make them easier to blend.

2. In a blender, combine the thawed cherries, ripe banana, almond butter, almond milk, and sweetener (if desired). Blend until you achieve a smooth and creamy consistency.

3. Pour the cherry-almond mixture into a clean CREAMi Pint, seal it with the storage lid, and place it in the freezer for approximately 2 hours. This short freezing time will help the mixture thicken into a creamy texture suitable for a smoothie bowl.

4. After the freezing time, take the CREAMi Pint out and remove the lid. Put the CREAMi pint in the outer bowl, ensuring the Creamerizer Paddle is attached onto the lid of the outer bowl, and lock.

5. Position the bowl components on the motor-base and secure by turning the handle to the right. Select the Smoothie Bowl function to create a smooth and creamy cherry almond base.

6. Once the machine has completed the process, serve your Cherry Almond Smoothie Bowl immediately. Top it with sliced almonds, fresh cherries,

granola, chia seeds, and a drizzle of honey for an extra touch of sweetness and crunch.

PREP TIP:

You can customize the sweetness by adjusting the amount of honey or maple syrup to suit your taste.

Lite Ice Creams

Low-Sugar Vanilla

SERVES 4

Enjoy the classic allure of vanilla ice cream with a healthier twist. Low-Sugar Vanilla Ice Cream is the perfect choice for those looking to satisfy their sweet tooth while keeping sugar in check. This recipe is specially crafted for the Ninja CREAMi.

PREP TIME: 10 minutes / Freeze time: 4 hours

FUNCTION: Ice Cream

TOOLS NEEDED: Mixing bowl, whisk or rubber spatula

Ingredients

- 2 cups of heavy cream
- 1 cup of whole milk
- 1/3 cup granulated sugar substitute (e.g., erythritol)
- 1 vanilla bean, split and seeds scraped
- 1 teaspoon pure vanilla extract

Instructions

1. Begin by combining the heavy cream, whole milk, and granulated sugar substitute in a mixing bowl. Stir until the sugar substitute is completely dissolved.

2. Add the scraped seeds from the vanilla bean and the pure vanilla extract to the mixture. Stir until thoroughly combined.

3. Transfer the mixture to a CREAMi Pint, seal it with the storage lid, and place it in the freezer for a minimum of 4 hours. The freezing time is crucial for achieving the desired creamy consistency while keeping sugar content low.

4. Once the freezing time has elapsed, remove the CREAMi Pint out of the freezer, then take off the lid. Put the CREAMi pint in the outer bowl. Ensure that the Creamerizer Paddle is attached to the outer bowl lid, and lock the lid assembly onto the outer bowl.

5. Position the bowl onto the base and turn the handle towards the right in order to secure it. Select the Ice Cream function to commence the churning process.

6. When the machine has completed churning, your Low-Sugar Vanilla Ice Cream is ready to be savored. Serve it immediately as is or garnish it with your preferred toppings.

PREP TIP:

For enhanced vanilla flavor, consider using two vanilla beans or a dash of additional pure vanilla extract.

Keto Chocolate

SERVES 4

Indulge in the rich, chocolatey goodness of Keto Chocolate Ice Cream without straying from your low-carb, high-fat diet. This recipe is tailored for keto enthusiasts and is perfectly suited for preparation using the Ninja CREAMi.

PREP TIME: 10 minutes / Freeze time: 4 hours

FUNCTION: Ice Cream

TOOLS NEEDED: Mixing bowl, whisk or rubber spatula

Ingredients

- 2 cups of heavy cream
- 1 cup unsweetened almond milk
- 1/3 cup granulated erythritol (or your preferred keto-friendly sweetener)
- 1/2 cup unsweetened cocoa powder
- 1 teaspoon pure vanilla extract

Instructions

1. In a bowl, mix the heavy cream, unsweetened almond milk, and granulated erythritol (or your chosen keto-friendly sweetener). Stir until the sweetener is fully dissolved.

2. Add the unsweetened cocoa powder and pure vanilla extract to the mixture. Stir until the ingredients are well incorporated.

3. Transfer the mixture to a CREAMi Pint, seal it with the storage lid, and place it in the freezer for a minimum of 4 hours. The freezing time is vital for achieving the creamy consistency while keeping carbohydrates to a minimum.

4. After the freezing period, retrieve the CREAMi Pint out of the freezer, then take off the lid. Put the CREAMi pint in the outer bowl. Ensure that the Creamerizer Paddle is attached to the outer bowl lid, and lock the lid assembly onto the outer bowl.

5. Position the bowl onto the base and turn the handle towards the right in order to secure it. Select the Ice Cream function to initiate the churning process.

6. Once the machine completes churning, your Keto Chocolate Ice Cream is ready to be enjoyed. Serve it immediately, or top it with your preferred keto-friendly toppings for an extra treat.

PREP TIP:

For a delightful twist, you can incorporate sugar-free chocolate chips or crushed nuts into the mixture before freezing.

Dairy-Free Strawberry

SERVES 4

Indulge in the refreshing taste of strawberries without the dairy. Dairy-Free Strawberry Ice Cream is a luscious and creamy treat perfect for those who prefer or require dairy-free options. This recipe is tailor-made for the Ninja CREAMi.

PREP TIME: 10 minutes / Freeze time: 4 hours

FUNCTION: Ice Cream

TOOLS NEEDED: Mixing bowl, whisk or rubber spatula

Ingredients

- 2 cups coconut milk (full-fat)

- 1 cup fresh or frozen strawberries, hulled and sliced

- 1/3 cup granulated sugar substitute (e.g., coconut sugar)

- 1 teaspoon pure vanilla extract

Instructions

1. In a mixing bowl, combine the full-fat coconut milk, sliced strawberries, granulated sugar substitute, and pure vanilla extract. Stir until the ingredients are well blended.

2. Transfer the mixture to a CREAMi Pint, seal it with the storage lid, and place it in the freezer for a minimum of 4 hours. Freezing allows the dairy-free ice cream to reach its desired creamy consistency.

3. After the freezing period, take the CREAMi Pint out and remove the lid. Put the CREAMi pint in the outer bowl. Ensure the Creamerizer Paddle is attached to the lid of the outer bowl and lock the assembly into place.

4. Position the bowl onto the base and turn the handle towards the right in order to secure it. Select the Ice Cream function to initiate the churning process.

5. Once the machine completes churning, your Dairy-Free Strawberry Ice Cream is ready to be enjoyed. Serve it immediately or embellish it with your favorite dairy-free toppings.

PREP TIP:

For added strawberry flavor, consider incorporating a few more sliced strawberries into the mixture.

Vegan Mint Chip

SERVES 4

Indulge in the refreshing and delightful flavor of Vegan Mint Chip Ice Cream. This dairy-free, egg-free rendition captures the essence of mint and the satisfying crunch of chocolate chips while maintaining a creamy texture. Perfectly tailored for the Ninja CREAMi.

PREP TIME: 10 minutes / Freeze time: 4 hours

FUNCTION: Ice Cream

TOOLS NEEDED: Mixing bowl, whisk or rubber spatula

Ingredients

- 2 cups coconut milk (full fat)
- 1/2 cup granulated sugar
- 1/2 teaspoon peppermint extract

- 1/2 cup vegan chocolate chips
- A few drops of green food coloring (optional)

Instructions

1. In a mixing bowl, combine the full-fat coconut milk and granulated sugar. Whip the sugar until completely dissolved.

2. Add the peppermint extract to the mixture and stir until well incorporated.

3. If desired, add a few drops of green food coloring to achieve the classic mint color. This step is optional but adds a delightful visual touch.

4. Transfer the mixture to a CREAMi Pint, seal it with the storage lid, and place it in the freezer for a minimum of 4 hours. The freezing period is essential for achieving the desired creamy texture.

5. Once the freezing time has passed, take the CREAMi Pint out and remove the lid. Put the CREAMi pint in the outer bowl. Ensure that the Creamerizer Paddle is attached to the outer bowl lid, and lock the lid assembly onto the outer bowl.

6. Position the bowl onto the base and turn the handle towards the right in order to secure it. Select the Ice Cream function to begin the churning process.

7. When the machine completes churning, your Vegan Mint Chip Ice Cream is ready to be enjoyed. Add the vegan chocolate chips during the last moments of churning, allowing them to be evenly distributed throughout the ice cream.

8. Serve immediately for a refreshing and dairy-free dessert experience.

PREP TIP:

For an even more intense mint flavor, you can adjust the peppermint extract to your taste preference.

Low-Fat Cookies and Cream

SERVES 4

Indulge in the classic combination of chocolate cookies and creamy ice cream while keeping it low in fat. Low-Fat Cookies and Cream Ice Cream is a guilt-free treat that doesn't skimp on flavor.

PREP TIME: 10 minutes / Freeze time: 4 hours

FUNCTION: Ice Cream

TOOLS NEEDED: Mixing bowl, whisk or rubber spatula

Ingredients

- 2 cups low-fat or fat-free vanilla yogurt
- 1 cup skim milk
- 1/2 cup granulated sugar
- 10 chocolate sandwich cookies, crushed

Instructions

1. In a mixing bowl, combine the low-fat or fat-free vanilla yogurt, skim milk, and granulated sugar. Whip the sugar until completely dissolved.

2. Add the crushed chocolate sandwich cookies to the mixture. Stir until the cookies are evenly distributed throughout the mixture.

3. Transfer the mixture to a CREAMi Pint, seal it with the storage lid, and place it in the freezer for a minimum of 4 hours. The freezing time allows the ice cream to set to the desired consistency.

4. After the freezing period, take the CREAMi Pint out and remove the lid. Put the CREAMi pint in the outer bowl. Ensure that the Creamerizer Paddle is

attached to the outer bowl lid, and lock the lid assembly onto the outer bowl.

5. Position the bowl onto the base and turn the handle towards the right in order to secure it. Select the Ice Cream function to initiate the churning process.

6. Once the churning is complete, your Low-Fat Cookies and Cream Ice Cream is ready to be enjoyed. Serve it immediately with your preferred toppings or savor its delicious simplicity on its own.

PREP TIP:

For added crunch, reserve some crushed cookies to sprinkle on top as a garnish.

Sugar-Free Raspberry

SERVES 4

Indulge in the vibrant flavors of summer with Sugar-Free Raspberry Ice Cream. This delightful dessert combines the sweet-tartness of ripe raspberries with the guilt-free goodness of a sugar-free recipe. It's the perfect treat for those watching their sugar intake and crafted for the Ninja CREAMi.

PREP TIME: 10 minutes / Freeze time: 4 hours

FUNCTION: Ice Cream

TOOLS NEEDED: Mixing bowl, whisk or rubber spatula

Ingredients

- 2 cups of heavy cream

- 1 cup of whole milk

- 1/3 cup sugar substitute (e.g., erythritol)
- 1 cup fresh raspberries
- 1 teaspoon pure vanilla extract
- 1 teaspoon lemon juice

Instructions

1. Begin by combining the heavy cream, whole milk, and sugar substitute in a mixing bowl. Stir until the sugar substitute is fully dissolved.

2. Add the fresh raspberries, pure vanilla extract, and lemon juice to the mixture. Use a whisk or rubber spatula to blend everything together until it forms a uniform mixture.

3. Transfer the raspberry-infused mixture to a CREAMi Pint, seal it with the storage lid, and place it in the freezer for a minimum of 4 hours. This freezing time is essential to achieve the desired creamy texture while keeping sugar content low.

4. After the freezing period, take the CREAMi Pint out and remove the lid. Put the CREAMi pint in the outer bowl. Ensure that the Creamerizer Paddle is attached to the outer bowl lid, and lock the lid assembly onto the outer bowl.

5. Position the bowl onto the base and turn the handle towards the right in order to secure it. Select the Ice Cream function to initiate the churning process.

6. Once the machine has completed churning, your Sugar-Free Raspberry Ice Cream is ready to be enjoyed. Serve it immediately or add some fresh raspberries for a burst of color and flavor.

PREP TIP:

For an extra hint of tartness, consider adding a few more fresh raspberries when serving.

Paleo Coconut

SERVES 4

Indulge in the delightful taste of coconut while staying true to your Paleo lifestyle with this creamy and satisfying Paleo Coconut Ice Cream. This recipe is tailored for use with the Ninja CREAMi.

PREP TIME: 10 minutes / Freeze time: 4 hours

FUNCTION: Ice Cream

TOOLS NEEDED: Mixing bowl, whisk or rubber spatula

Ingredients

- 2 cups full-fat coconut milk
- 1/2 cup unsweetened shredded coconut
- 1/3 cup honey or maple syrup (adjust to taste)
- 1 teaspoon pure vanilla extract

Instructions

1. In a mixing bowl, combine the full-fat coconut milk, unsweetened shredded coconut, honey (or maple syrup), and pure vanilla extract. Stir until the ingredients are well incorporated.

2. Transfer the mixture to a CREAMi Pint, seal it with the storage lid, and place it in the freezer for a minimum of 4 hours. Freezing is essential to achieve the desired creamy texture while adhering to Paleo principles.

3. After the freezing period, take the CREAMi Pint out and remove the lid. Put the CREAMi pint in the outer bowl. Ensure that the Creamerizer Paddle is

attached to the outer bowl lid, and lock the lid assembly onto the outer bowl.

4. Position the bowl onto the base and turn the handle towards the right in order to secure it. Select the Ice Cream function to initiate the churning process.

5. When the machine has completed churning, your Paleo Coconut Ice Cream is ready to be enjoyed. Serve it immediately or top it with additional shredded coconut for extra flavor and texture.

PREP TIP:

For a more intense coconut flavor, consider toasting the shredded coconut lightly before adding it to the mixture.

Low-Carb Lemon

SERVES 4

Indulge in the zesty goodness of Low-Carb Lemon Ice Cream. This delightful frozen treat is a perfect choice for those watching their carb intake while craving a burst of citrusy flavor. Crafted for the Ninja CREAMi.

PREP TIME: 10 minutes / Freeze time: 4 hours

FUNCTION: Ice Cream

TOOLS NEEDED: Mixing bowl, whisk or rubber spatula

Ingredients

- 2 cups of heavy cream

- 1 cup of whole milk

- 1/3 cup granulated sugar substitute (e.g., erythritol)

- Zest and juice of 2 lemons

- 1 teaspoon pure vanilla extract

Instructions

1. Start by combining the heavy cream, whole milk, and granulated sugar substitute in a mixing bowl. Stir until the sugar substitute is fully dissolved.

2. Add the zest and juice from the lemons, along with the pure vanilla extract, to the mixture. Stir thoroughly to ensure even distribution of the lemony goodness.

3. Transfer the mixture to a CREAMi Pint, seal it with the storage lid, and place it in the freezer for a minimum of 4 hours. The freezing time is essential for achieving the desired creamy texture while keeping carbs in check.

4. After the freezing period, take the CREAMi Pint out and remove the lid. Put the CREAMi pint in the outer bowl. Ensure that the Creamerizer Paddle is attached to the outer bowl lid, and lock the lid assembly onto the outer bowl.

5. Position the bowl onto the base and turn the handle towards the right in order to secure it. Select the Ice Cream function to initiate the churning process.

6. When the machine has finished churning, your Low-Carb Lemon Ice Cream is ready to be enjoyed. Serve it immediately with your choice of low-carb toppings, or enjoy it as a refreshing standalone treat.

PREP TIP:

For extra lemony zest, consider adding a touch more lemon juice or zest to suit your taste.

Gluten-Free Brownie Batter

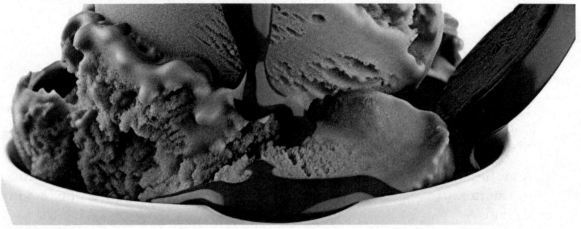

SERVES 4

Indulge your sweet tooth with the rich and decadent flavors of Gluten-Free Brownie Batter Ice Cream. This delightful dessert combines the irresistible taste of brownie batter with the creamy goodness of ice cream. Best of all, it's gluten-free!

PREP TIME: 15 minutes / Freeze time: 4 hours

FUNCTION: Ice Cream

TOOLS NEEDED: Mixing bowl, whisk or rubber spatula

Ingredients

- 2 cups of heavy cream
- 1 cup of whole milk
- 1/2 cup gluten-free brownie mix
- 1/4 cup unsweetened cocoa powder
- 1/3 cup granulated sugar
- 1 teaspoon pure vanilla extract

Instructions

1. In a bowl, mix the heavy cream, whole milk, gluten-free brownie mix, unsweetened cocoa powder, and granulated sugar. Stir until all the dry ingredients are fully incorporated into the mixture.

2. Add the pure vanilla extract to the mixture and continue to stir until well combined.

3. Transfer the mixture to a CREAMi Pint, seal it with the storage lid, and place it in the freezer for a minimum of 4 hours. Freezing the mixture allows it to achieve the perfect ice cream consistency while preserving its gluten-free status.

4. After the freezing period, take the CREAMi Pint out and remove the lid. Put the CREAMi pint in the outer bowl. Ensure that the Creamerizer Paddle is attached to the outer bowl lid, and lock the lid assembly onto the outer bowl.

5. Position the bowl onto the base and turn the handle towards the right in order to secure it. Select the Ice Cream function to begin churning.

6. Once the machine completes the churning process, your Gluten-Free Brownie Batter Ice Cream is ready to be enjoyed. Serve it immediately as a delectable treat or indulge in it with your favorite gluten-free brownie chunks mixed in.

PREP TIP:

For an added burst of chocolatey goodness, consider adding gluten-free brownie chunks to the ice cream mixture before freezing.

Weight Watchers Peach

SERVES 4

Indulge in the luscious sweetness of peaches while keeping your health goals on track with this Weight Watchers Peach Ice Cream. It's a delightful guilt-free treat specially designed for the Ninja CREAMi.

PREP TIME: 10 minutes / Freeze time: 4 hours

FUNCTION: Ice Cream

TOOLS NEEDED: Mixing bowl, whisk or rubber spatula

Ingredients

- 2 cups fresh ripe peaches, peeled and diced
- 2 tablespoons lemon juice
- 1/2 cup non-fat Greek yogurt
- 1/4 cup granulated sugar substitute (e.g., Stevia)
- 1 teaspoon pure vanilla extract

Instructions

1. In a mixing bowl, combine the diced peaches and lemon juice. Toss gently to coat the peaches with the lemon juice, which enhances their natural flavor.

2. Add the non-fat Greek yogurt, granulated sugar substitute, and pure vanilla extract to the bowl. Stir until all the ingredients are thoroughly mixed.

3. Transfer the peach mixture to a blender or food processor and blend until you achieve a smooth puree.

4. Pour the peach puree into a CREAMi Pint, seal it with the storage lid, and place it in the freezer for a minimum of 4 hours. This chilling period allows the flavors to meld and the texture to become delightfully creamy.

5. Once the freezing time has elapsed, remove the CREAMi Pint out of the freezer, then take off the lid. Put the CREAMi pint in the outer bowl, ensuring that the Creamerizer Paddle is attached onto the lid of the outer bowl, and lock.

6. Position the bowl onto the base and turn the handle towards the right in order to secure it. Select the Ice Cream function to initiate the churning process.

7. When the machine completes churning, your Weight Watchers Peach Ice Cream is ready to be enjoyed. Serve it immediately, relishing the delightful fusion of peachy goodness and guilt-free satisfaction.

PREP TIP:

For a touch of added sweetness, consider a drizzle of honey or a sprinkle of your preferred sugar substitute just before serving.

Lite Chocolate Cookie Ice Cream

SERVES 4

Indulge in the guilt-free pleasure of Lite Chocolate Cookie Ice Cream. This lighter version of a classic favorite offers all the delightful chocolatey goodness without the extra calories. It's a treat you can enjoy without hesitation.

PREP TIME: 15 minutes / Freeze time: 4 hours

FUNCTION: Ice Cream

TOOLS NEEDED: Mixing bowl, whisk or rubber spatula

Ingredients

- 2 cups light whipped topping (e.g., Cool Whip)
- 1 cup skim milk
- 1/4 cup unsweetened cocoa powder
- 1/3 cup granulated sugar
- 1 teaspoon pure vanilla extract
- 1/2 cup crushed chocolate sandwich cookies (lite or reduced-fat)

Instructions

1. In a mixing bowl, combine the light whipped topping, skim milk, unsweetened cocoa powder, granulated sugar, and pure vanilla extract. Stir until the ingredients are thoroughly mixed and the sugar has dissolved.

2. Gently fold in the crushed chocolate sandwich cookies, distributing them evenly throughout the mixture.

3. Transfer the mixture to a CREAMi Pint and secure the lid. Freeze for a minimum of 4 hours, allowing the ice cream to set and develop its creamy texture.

4. After the freezing period, remove the CREAMi Pint out of the freezer, then take off the lid. Put the CREAMi pint in the outer bowl, ensuring the Creamerizer Paddle is attached onto the lid of the outer bowl, and lock.

5. Position the bowl onto the base and turn the handle towards the right in order to secure it. Select the Ice Cream function to begin churning.

6. Once the churning process is complete, your Lite Chocolate Cookie Ice Cream is ready to savor. Serve it immediately and enjoy the delightful combination of chocolate and cookies without the guilt.

PREP TIP:

For a variation, consider adding a drizzle of sugar-free chocolate syrup before serving.

Lite Raspberry Ice Cream

SERVES 4

Indulge in the refreshing and tangy goodness of Lite Raspberry Ice Cream. This guilt-free treat is light on calories but heavy on flavor, making it the perfect choice for a delightful dessert.

PREP TIME: 15 minutes / Freeze time: 4 hours

FUNCTION: Ice Cream

TOOLS NEEDED: Mixing bowl, whisk or rubber spatula

Ingredients

- 2 cups non-fat Greek yogurt

- 1 cup fresh raspberries

- 1/2 cup honey or agave nectar

- 1 teaspoon pure vanilla extract

- 1/4 cup raspberry sauce (optional, for swirl)

Instructions

1. In a mixing bowl, combine the non-fat Greek yogurt, fresh raspberries, honey (or agave nectar), and pure vanilla extract. Stir until the mixture is smooth and the honey is fully incorporated.

2. If desired, add the raspberry sauce to create a beautiful swirl effect. Gently fold it into the yogurt mixture.

3. Transfer the raspberry yogurt mixture to a CREAMi Pint and secure the lid. Freeze for a minimum of 4 hours to allow the flavors to meld and the ice cream to firm up.

4. After the freezing period, take the CREAMi Pint out of the freezer, then take off the lid. Put the CREAMi pint in the outer bowl, ensuring the Creamerizer Paddle is attached onto the lid of the outer bowl, and lock.

5. Position the bowl assembly on the motor base and twist the handle to the right to raise the platform and lock it in place. Select the Ice Cream function to start the churning process.

6. Once the churning is complete, your Lite Raspberry Ice Cream is ready to be savored. Serve it immediately for a delightful and guilt-free dessert.

PREP TIP:

For added freshness, consider garnishing with a few extra fresh raspberries before serving.

Lite Peanut Butter Ice Cream

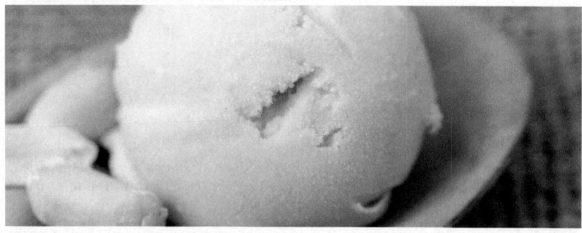

SERVES 4

Indulge your cravings without the guilt with this Lite Peanut Butter Ice Cream. It's a creamy and dreamy dessert that combines the richness of peanut butter with a lighter touch, making it perfect for those looking for a healthier treat.

PREP TIME: 15 minutes / Freeze time: 4 hours

FUNCTION: Ice Cream

TOOLS NEEDED: Mixing bowl, whisk or rubber spatula

Ingredients

- 2 cups fat-free Greek yogurt
- 1/2 cup creamy peanut butter
- 1/2 cup powdered sugar
- 1 teaspoon pure vanilla extract
- 1/4 cup roasted unsalted peanuts, chopped

Instructions

1. In a mixing bowl, combine the fat-free Greek yogurt, creamy peanut butter, powdered sugar, and pure vanilla extract. Stir until the mixture is smooth and well incorporated.

2. Gently fold in the chopped roasted unsalted peanuts to add a delightful crunch and extra peanut flavor.

3. Transfer the peanut butter mixture to a CREAMi Pint and secure the lid. Freeze for a minimum of 4 hours, allowing the ice cream to set and achieve a creamy texture.

4. After the freezing period, take the CREAMi Pint out and remove the lid. Put the CREAMi pint in the outer bowl, ensuring the Creamerizer Paddle is attached onto the lid of the outer bowl, and lock.

5. Position the bowl onto the base and turn the handle towards the right in order to secure it. Select the Ice Cream function to begin churning.

6. Once the churning process is complete, your Lite Peanut Butter Ice Cream is ready to enjoy. It's a guilt-free indulgence that's sure to satisfy your peanut butter cravings.

PREP TIP:

For added flair, drizzle a touch of honey or a sprinkle of mini chocolate chips on top before serving.

Mix-in Creations

Rocky Road

SERVES 4

Rocky Road Ice Cream is the perfect marriage of rich chocolate, crunchy nuts, and fluffy marshmallows. This recipe elevates this classic flavor to a new level of creaminess, creating a delightful frozen treat.

PREP TIME: 15 minutes / Freeze time: 4 hours

FUNCTION: Ice Cream

TOOLS NEEDED: Mixing bowl, whisk or rubber spatula

Ingredients

- 2 cups of heavy cream
- 1 cup of whole milk
- 3/4 cup of granulated sugar
- 1/2 cup unsweetened cocoa powder
- 1/2 cup mini marshmallows
- 1/2 cup chopped almonds
- 1/4 cup mini chocolate chips

Instructions

1. Combine in a mixing bowl the heavy cream, granulated sugar, whole milk, and unsweetened cocoa powder. Stir until the sugar and cocoa powder are fully dissolved.

2. Add the mini marshmallows, chopped almonds, and mini chocolate chips to the mixture. Stir until all the ingredients are evenly distributed.

3. Transfer the mixture to a CREAMi Pint, seal it with the storage lid, and place it in the freezer for a minimum of 4 hours. This freezing period allows the flavors to meld and the texture to become wonderfully creamy.

4. After the freezing time, take the CREAMi Pint out and remove the lid. Put the CREAMi pint in the outer bowl, ensuring the Creamerizer Paddle is attached onto the lid of the outer bowl, and lock.

5. Position the bowl onto the base and turn the handle towards the right in order to secure it. Select the Ice Cream function to begin churning.

6. As soon as the churning process is completed, your Rocky Road Ice Cream is ready to be savored. Serve it immediately, and relish the delightful combination of chocolatey indulgence, crunchy almonds, and fluffy marshmallows.

PREP TIP:

Feel free to customize your Rocky Road Ice Cream by adding more marshmallows, almonds, or chocolate chips to suit your taste.

Birthday Cake

SERVES 4

There's no better way to celebrate than with a scoop of Birthday Cake Ice Cream. This delightful concoction captures the essence of a birthday cake in a creamy frozen treat. It's a party in every spoonful!

PREP TIME: 15 minutes / Freeze time: 4 hours

FUNCTION: Ice Cream

TOOLS NEEDED: Mixing bowl, whisk or rubber spatula

Ingredients

- 2 cups of heavy cream
- 1 cup of whole milk
- 3/4 cup of granulated sugar
- 1 teaspoon pure vanilla extract
- 1/2 cup rainbow sprinkles
- 1/2 cup crushed birthday cake-flavored cookies

Instructions

1. In a bowl, mix the heavy cream, whole milk, and granulated sugar. Whip the sugar until completely dissolved.

2. Add the pure vanilla extract to the mixture and stir until well combined.

3. Gently fold in the rainbow sprinkles and crushed birthday cake-flavored cookies to infuse the classic birthday cake flavors.

4. Transfer the mixture to a CREAMi Pint and secure the lid. Freeze for at least 4 hours, allowing the flavors to meld and the ice cream to achieve its signature creamy texture.

5. After the freezing period, retrieve the CREAMi Pint out of the freezer, then take off the lid. Put the CREAMi pint in the outer bowl, ensuring the Creamerizer Paddle is attached onto the lid of the outer bowl, and lock.

6. Position the bowl onto the base and turn the handle towards the right in order to secure it. Select the Ice Cream function to begin churning.

7. Once the churning process is complete, your Birthday Cake Ice Cream is ready to delight taste buds. Serve it immediately, and let the celebration begin!

PREP TIP:

For an extra festive touch, garnish with additional rainbow sprinkles before serving.

S'mores

SERVES 4

Indulge in the nostalgic flavors of a campfire classic with S'mores Ice Cream. This delightful frozen treat captures the essence of gooey marshmallows, rich chocolate, and crunchy graham crackers, all in one creamy scoop.

PREP TIME: 15 minutes / Freeze time: 4 hours

FUNCTION: Ice Cream

TOOLS NEEDED: Mixing bowl, whisk or rubber spatula

Ingredients

- 2 cups of heavy cream
- 1 cup of whole milk
- 3/4 cup of granulated sugar
- 1 teaspoon pure vanilla extract
- 1/2 cup mini marshmallows
- 1/2 cup chopped milk chocolate or chocolate chips
- 1/2 cup crushed graham crackers

Instructions

1. In a bowl, mix the heavy cream, whole milk, and granulated sugar. Whip the sugar until completely dissolved.

2. Add the pure vanilla extract to the mixture and stir until well combined.

3. Gently fold in the mini marshmallows, chopped milk chocolate (or chocolate chips), and crushed graham crackers to recreate the signature S'mores flavor.

4. Transfer the mixture to a CREAMi Pint and secure the lid. Freeze for at least 4 hours, allowing the flavors to meld and the ice cream to achieve its characteristic creaminess.

5. After the freezing period, retrieve the CREAMi Pint out of the freezer, then take off the lid. Put the CREAMi pint in the outer bowl, ensuring the Creamerizer Paddle is attached onto the lid of the outer bowl, and lock.

6. Position the bowl onto the base and turn the handle towards the right in order to secure it. Select the Ice Cream function to begin churning.

7. Once the churning process is complete, your S'mores Ice Cream is ready to transport you back to the campfire. Serve it immediately and enjoy the flavors of the great outdoors.

PREP TIP:

For an extra toasty flavor, you can briefly torch the marshmallows with a kitchen torch before adding them to the mixture.

Apple Pie

SERVES 4

Indulge in the warm and comforting flavors of apple pie with this delightful Apple Pie Ice Cream. It's like having a slice of pie in frozen form, complete with chunks of spiced apples and a buttery crust swirl.

PREP TIME: 20 minutes / Freeze time: 4 hours

FUNCTION: Ice Cream

TOOLS NEEDED: Mixing bowl, whisk or rubber spatula

Ingredients

- 2 cups of heavy cream
- 1 cup of whole milk
- 3/4 cup of granulated sugar
- 1 teaspoon ground cinnamon
- 1/4 teaspoon ground nutmeg
- 1 1/2 cups diced and cooked apples (cooked with sugar and a dash of cinnamon)
- 1/2 cup crushed pie crust pieces

Instructions

1. Combine in a mixing bowl the heavy cream, granulated sugar, whole milk , ground cinnamon, and ground nutmeg. Whip the sugar until completely dissolved.

2. Gently fold in the diced and cooked apples, ensuring they are evenly distributed throughout the mixture.

3. Add the crushed pie crust pieces to infuse that wonderful crust flavor into the ice cream.

4. Transfer the mixture to a CREAMi Pint and secure the lid. Freeze for at least 4 hours, allowing the ice cream to take on the essence of a homemade apple pie.

5. After the freezing period, retrieve the CREAMi Pint out of the freezer, then take off the lid. Put the CREAMi pint in the outer bowl, ensuring the Creamerizer Paddle is attached onto the lid of the outer bowl, and lock.

6. Position the bowl onto the base and turn the handle towards the right in order to secure it. Select the Ice Cream function to begin churning.

7. Once the churning process is complete, your Apple Pie Ice Cream is ready to be enjoyed. Serve it immediately, and savor the comforting flavors of apple pie in every spoonful.

PREP TIP:

To cook the apples, simply sauté them in a pan with a bit of sugar and a dash of cinnamon until they are tender.

Caramel Swirl

SERVES 4

Indulge in the sweet, velvety goodness of Caramel Swirl Ice Cream. This exquisite frozen treat marries the richness of caramel with the creaminess of ice cream. It's a delightful swirl of flavors that will leave you craving more.

PREP TIME: 15 minutes / Freeze time: 4 hours

FUNCTION: Ice Cream

TOOLS NEEDED: Mixing bowl, whisk or rubber spatula

Ingredients

- 2 cups of heavy cream
- 1 cup of whole milk
- 3/4 cup of granulated sugar
- 1/2 cup caramel sauce, plus extra for swirling
- 1 teaspoon pure vanilla extract

Instructions

1. In a bowl, mix the heavy cream, whole milk, and granulated sugar. Whip the sugar until completely dissolved.

2. Add the pure vanilla extract to the mixture and stir until well combined.

3. Pour in the caramel sauce and gently stir to infuse the rich caramel flavor throughout the base.

4. Transfer the mixture to a CREAMi Pint and secure the lid. Freeze for a minimum of 4 hours, allowing the caramel to meld with the ice cream, creating the perfect swirl.

5. After the freezing period, take the CREAMi Pint out of the freezer, then take off the lid. Put the CREAMi pint in the outer bowl, ensuring the Creamerizer Paddle is attached onto the lid of the outer bowl, and lock.

6. Position the bowl onto the base and turn the handle towards the right in order to secure it. Select the Ice Cream function to commence the churning process.

7. Once the churning is complete, your Caramel Swirl Ice Cream is ready to be savored. Serve it immediately, drizzling extra caramel sauce for that irresistible swirl effect.

PREP TIP:

For a more intense caramel flavor, consider adding chopped caramel candies or caramelized nuts as mix-ins.

Mocha Crunch

SERVES 4

Indulge in the rich and invigorating flavors of Mocha Crunch Ice Cream. This coffee-infused delight combines the boldness of espresso with the satisfying crunch of chocolate-covered espresso beans.

PREP TIME: 15 minutes / Freeze time: 4 hours

FUNCTION: Ice Cream

TOOLS NEEDED: Mixing bowl, whisk or rubber spatula

Ingredients

- 2 cups of heavy cream
- 1 cup of whole milk
- 3/4 cup of granulated sugar
- 2 tablespoons instant espresso powder
- 1/2 cup chocolate-covered espresso beans, roughly chopped

Instructions

1. In a bowl, mix the heavy cream, whole milk, and granulated sugar. Whip the sugar until completely dissolved.

2. Add the instant espresso powder to the mixture and stir until well combined. This is where the robust coffee flavor comes to life.

3. Gently fold in the roughly chopped chocolate-covered espresso beans. This step introduces a delightful crunch and intense chocolate notes to the ice cream.

4. Transfer the mixture to a CREAMi Pint and secure the lid. Freeze for at least 4 hours, allowing the flavors to meld and the ice cream to achieve a creamy yet crunchy texture.

5. After the freezing time, remove the CREAMi Pint out of the freezer, then take off the lid. Put the CREAMi pint in the outer bowl, ensuring the Creamerizer Paddle is attached onto the lid of the outer bowl, and lock.

6. Position the bowl onto the base and turn the handle towards the right in order to secure it. Select the Ice Cream function to begin churning.

7. Once the churning process is complete, your Mocha Crunch Ice Cream is ready to awaken your senses. Serve it immediately and savor the perfect blend of coffee and chocolate crunch.

PREP TIP:

For a stronger coffee flavor, you can adjust the amount of instant espresso powder to your preference.

Peanut Butter Cup

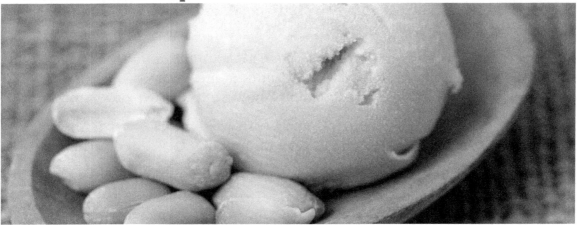

SERVES 4

Indulge in the creamy delight of Peanut Butter Cup Ice Cream. This recipe combines the irresistible flavors of rich peanut butter and chocolate, creating a frozen treat that's a true peanut butter lover's dream.

PREP TIME: 15 minutes / Freeze time: 4 hours

FUNCTION: Ice Cream

TOOLS NEEDED: Mixing bowl, whisk or rubber spatula

Ingredients

- 2 cups of heavy cream
- 1 cup of whole milk
- 3/4 cup of granulated sugar
- 1/2 cup smooth peanut butter
- 1/2 cup chopped peanut butter cups (miniature size)
- 1/4 cup chocolate fudge sauce

Instructions

1. In a bowl, mix the heavy cream, whole milk, and granulated sugar. Whip the sugar until completely dissolved.

2. Add the smooth peanut butter to the mixture and stir until well combined, infusing the ice cream base with rich peanut flavor.

3. Gently fold in the chopped peanut butter cups to add delightful chocolate and peanut butter surprises throughout the ice cream.

4. Transfer the mixture to a CREAMi Pint and secure the lid. Freeze for at least 4 hours, allowing the flavors to meld and the ice cream to reach its perfect consistency.

5. After the freezing period, remove the CREAMi Pint out of the freezer, then take off the lid. Put the CREAMi pint in the outer bowl, ensuring the Creamerizer Paddle is attached onto the lid of the outer bowl, and lock.

6. Position the bowl onto the base and turn the handle towards the right in order to secure it. Select the Ice Cream function to begin churning.

7. Once the churning process is complete, your Peanut Butter Cup Ice Cream is ready to be savored. Drizzle chocolate fudge sauce over each serving for an extra indulgent touch.

PREP TIP:

For added crunch and peanut butter cup goodness, consider reserving some chopped peanut butter cups to sprinkle on top as a garnish.

Snickerdoodle

SERVES 4

Indulge in the sweet, cinnamon-infused delight of Snickerdoodle Ice Cream. This creamy creation captures the essence of the beloved cookie in frozen form, complete with swirls of cinnamon sugar.

PREP TIME: 15 minutes / Freeze time: 4 hours

FUNCTION: Ice Cream

TOOLS NEEDED: Mixing bowl, whisk or rubber spatula

Ingredients

- 2 cups of heavy cream

- 1 cup of whole milk

- 3/4 cup of granulated sugar

- 1 teaspoon ground cinnamon

- 1/2 cup crushed Snickerdoodle cookies

- 1/4 cup cinnamon sugar (for swirl)

Instructions

1. Combine in a mixing bowl the heavy cream, granulated sugar, whole milk , and ground cinnamon. Whip the sugar until completely dissolved.

2. Gently fold in the crushed Snickerdoodle cookies to infuse that unmistakable cookie flavor into the ice cream base.

3. Transfer the mixture to a CREAMi Pint and secure the lid. Freeze for at least 4 hours, allowing the flavors to meld and the ice cream to achieve its signature creamy texture.

4. After the freezing period, retrieve the CREAMi Pint out of the freezer, then take off the lid. Put the CREAMi pint in the outer bowl, ensuring the Creamerizer Paddle is attached onto the lid of the outer bowl, and lock.

5. Position the bowl onto the base and turn the handle towards the right in order to secure it. Select the Ice Cream function to begin churning.

6. As the ice cream churns, periodically sprinkle layers of cinnamon sugar into the mixture to create cinnamon sugar swirls throughout the ice cream.

7. Once the churning process is complete, your Snickerdoodle Ice Cream is ready to enjoy. Serve it immediately, reveling in the cinnamon-kissed goodness.

PREP TIP:

For an extra layer of cinnamon flavor, sprinkle some extra ground cinnamon over the ice cream before serving.

Maple Walnut

SERVES 4

Indulge in the rich and comforting flavors of Maple Walnut Ice Cream. This delightful frozen treat combines the earthy sweetness of maple syrup with the satisfying crunch of toasted walnuts, creating a harmonious blend of textures and tastes.

PREP TIME: 15 minutes / Freeze time: 4 hours

FUNCTION: Ice Cream

TOOLS NEEDED: Mixing bowl, whisk or rubber spatula

Ingredients

- 2 cups of heavy cream
- 1 cup of whole milk
- 3/4 cup of granulated sugar
- 1/2 cup pure maple syrup
- 1/2 cup chopped toasted walnuts

Instructions

1. In a bowl, mix the heavy cream, whole milk, and granulated sugar. Whip the sugar until completely dissolved.

2. Add the pure maple syrup to the mixture and stir until well combined. The maple syrup will infuse the ice cream with its distinctive and comforting flavor.

3. Gently fold in the chopped toasted walnuts, distributing them evenly throughout the mixture for a delightful crunch in every bite.

4. Transfer the mixture to a CREAMi Pint and secure the lid. Freeze for a minimum of 4 hours to allow the flavors to meld and the ice cream to attain its signature creamy texture.

5. After the freezing period, take out the CREAMi Pint out of the freezer, then take off the lid. Put the CREAMi pint in the outer bowl, ensuring the Creamerizer Paddle is attached onto the lid of the outer bowl, and lock.

6. Position the bowl onto the base and turn the handle towards the right in order to secure it. Select the Ice Cream function to begin churning.

7. Once the churning process is complete, your Maple Walnut Ice Cream is ready to be enjoyed. Serve it immediately, savoring the harmonious blend of maple sweetness and nutty crunch.

PREP TIP:

For an even richer flavor, consider using Grade A dark amber maple syrup.

Cookie Dough

SERVES 4

Indulge in the delightful combination of creamy ice cream and chunks of cookie dough. This Cookie Dough Ice Cream recipe is a crowd-pleaser, perfect for satisfying your sweet tooth.

PREP TIME: 15 minutes / Freeze time: 4 hours

FUNCTION: Ice Cream

TOOLS NEEDED: Mixing bowl, whisk or rubber spatula

Ingredients

- 2 cups of heavy cream

- 1 cup of whole milk

- 3/4 cup of granulated sugar

- 1 teaspoon pure vanilla extract

- 1/2 cup chocolate chip cookie dough, cut into small chunks

Instructions

1. Begin by combining the heavy cream, whole milk, and granulated sugar in a mixing bowl. Stir until the sugar is completely dissolved.

2. Add the pure vanilla extract to the mixture and stir until well incorporated.

3. Gently fold in the chunks of chocolate chip cookie dough, ensuring they are evenly distributed throughout the mixture.

4. Transfer the mixture to a CREAMi Pint and seal it with the storage lid. Place the pint in the freezer for at least 4 hours to allow the ice cream to firm up and the flavors to meld.

5. After the freezing period, take the CREAMi Pint out and remove the lid. Put the CREAMi pint in the outer bowl, making sure the Creamerizer Paddle is attached onto the lid of the outer bowl, and lock.

6. Position the bowl components on the motor-base and secure by turning the handle to the right. Select the Ice Cream function to begin the churning process.

7. Once the churning is complete, your Cookie Dough Ice Cream is ready to be enjoyed. Serve it immediately, savoring the sweet combination of creamy ice cream and chunks of cookie dough in every bite.

PREP TIP:

For a more pronounced cookie dough flavor, consider using cookie dough with larger chunks.

Conclusion

In wrapping up this culinary journey, it's evident that the recipes presented here offer a delightful array of flavors and textures to tantalize your taste buds. From the timeless elegance of Classic Vanilla Ice Cream to the indulgent richness of Chocolate Fudge Ice Cream, the refreshing sweetness of Strawberry Swirl Ice Cream, the cool and invigorating Mint Chocolate Chip Ice Cream, and the irresistible charm of Cookies and Cream Ice Cream, you've explored a diverse spectrum of frozen treats.

Each recipe is designed with simplicity and taste in mind, ensuring that even novice chefs can achieve impressive results. Whether you're catering to family gatherings, entertaining guests, or simply treating yourself to a moment of culinary pleasure, these recipes have you covered.

In closing, these recipes offer not just delicious desserts but also the opportunity to explore your culinary creativity. Whether you're serving them at a gathering or savoring them in solitude, these frozen treats are sure to create moments of joy and satisfaction. So, get ready to embark on your own ice cream adventure and enjoy the sweet rewards of your kitchen endeavors!

Recipe Index

Printed in Great Britain
by Amazon

33322213R00099